LIFETIME TREASURY OF TESTED TENNIS TIPS:

Secrets of Winning Play

Bill Murphy and Chet Murphy

Illustrations by Dave Fitzsimmons

PARKER PUBLISHING COMPANY, INC.
WEST NYACK, NEW YORK

20   19   18   17   16   15   14   13   12   11

To
Our Wives,
Mimi
and
Pat

Reward Edition . . . . . . March 1981

Library of Congress Cataloging in Publication Data

Murphy, William E
  Lifetime treasury of tested tennis tips.

  1. Tennis.   I. Murphy, Chester W., joint author.
II. Title.
GV995.M847   796.34'22   77-17048

Foreword

Because of the recent spectacular growth in tennis, bookshelves throughout the country abound with newly published works on the game. Stroke mechanics, practice procedures, psychological factors, mental aspects—these and a host of other facets of the game have been covered excellently by well-qualified authors. Then why *another* book on the game?

The reason becomes obvious when one thumbs through the pages of this book. Bill and Chet Murphy have come up with a cleverly arranged, simply written how-to-do-it book that is different from all others. Covering virtually all facets of the game, they present ingenious tips and cues that are certain to be a boon to all tennis players. Through the use of catchy picture words and simple analogies and concepts, they make it easy for anyone to understand and to apply the basic principles behind correct technique.

Open the book to any page and you'll find a concise explanation of a tip or cue that will interest you. So simply explained are these tips and cues you'll want to rush out to a court and try them. Do it! They'll work for you.

Tony Trabert
Captain
U.S. Davis Cup Team

By
BILL AND CHET MURPHY
Tennis for Beginners
The Tennis Handbook
Tennis for Player, Teacher, and Coach

By
BILL MURPHY
The Complete Book of Championship Tennis Drills
Group Instruction in Tennis

By
CHET MURPHY
Advanced Tennis

We have been teaching and coaching tennis for the major parts of our lifetimes. During those many years we have introduced hundreds of youngsters to the game and have become their instructors. Now most of them continue to play as adults, and many of them bring their children to us for the same sound training they themselves had as youngsters. We consider this both a compliment and a privilege; a compliment because it attests to the effectiveness of our teaching methods, and a privilege because it offers us continued opportunities to extol the values of tennis as a lifetime recreational activity.

Tennis is one of the few sports that can be enjoyed by players of all ages. We know many six- and seven-year old boys and girls who play regularly; we also know several sixty- and seventy-year old players, most of whom have been playing since their teen years. Truly, tennis is *the* sport for a lifetime. Now here is a book for your lifetime of tennis.

Regardless of when you started to play and regardless of your present age and your playing ability, you can benefit from this book. In it we list more than two hundred tips to improve your game. Admittedly, this is far too many for you to remember or to apply at any particular time. But, by referring to this book at intervals between sessions on the courts, you will find solutions to various specific problems you encounter in your game. We intend this book to be used in this way—as a lifetime reference for tennis tips.

As a student of the game (you are a student or you wouldn't be reading this book), you should understand that it takes time to learn the strokes and shots necessary for successful play—not just the passage of time but time spent on the court in practice and play. And, if you are like most students, most of your practice and play will be done on your own, without the help of an instructor or coach. Though having to fend for yourself like this might seem to be a difficult way to learn, it really isn't. Many top-ranked players learned to play in exactly that way.

You too can learn on your own, using this treasury. Here we describe and illustrate many tips, cues, analogies, concepts, and gimmicks that will help you visualize yourself making the various strokes and shots of the game. The tips and cues will help you analyze strokes so that you become aware of the important parts of them and can work to develop them in your practice. This is not to say you must understand every mechanical detail of a stroke, and that you must constantly think about these details as you play or practice. Any attempt to do so would be disastrous just as it was for the legendary centipede who tried to analyze and concentrate on how he coordinated the movements of his numerous legs.

But still, you must know what the stroke feels like, either in its entirety or at some specific point, and you should know how to make it feel that way. The tips and cues we offer here will help you do that.

Many of our tips and cues are presented as simple analogies. We ask you to visualize yourself making a "candy-cane" swing, for example, or "playing patty-cake" with the ball, or "swinging along a railroad track." Such simple, yet vivid, images can be recalled easily and reviewed often; you can practice them on the court and can mentally rehearse them when you are away from the court.

This mental rehearsal does not take the place of actual physical practice, however. True, our tips and cues will help you "get the picture" of what is to be done, and as you see yourself performing—in your mind's eye—you will already have begun to learn the stroke or shot. But only through repeated attempts to hit as you intend to can you develop the sensitivity you need in your hand, wrist, and forearm to hit correctly. Only through practice can you develop the feel, the kinesthetic sense, necessary to handle the racket properly for the various strokes and play situations that arise.

But good strokes alone do not win tennis matches. You must know how and when to use your strokes to best advantage. For this purpose we include several tips on tactics and strategy and on practice procedures for learning sound tactics and strategy. Planning your net approach from the "green" of two-color courts and hitting with a planned margin of safety are examples of useful tips on tactics.

Many of our tips and cues may seem too simple to be effective. Don't be misled by this. Most successful teachers and coaches rely on such simple procedures to make their teaching effective. They know that when a learner understands what is to be done he is properly on his way to learning how to do it. They also know that a universally effective way to help a student is to relate the learning problem to some past experience of the student. "Swing as in baseball," "fling a frisbee," "spin a top," "serve like a thrower"—these are all simple ways to relate previously learned skills to the skills of tennis. Tips and cues such as these are the core of this book. They have worked for thousands of our students. Try them; they'll work for you, too.

Bill and Chet Murphy

Contents

CONTENTS

CONTENTS

CONTENTS

GROUND STROKES

Unless you are well beyond the intermediate level of play, more than 75% of the shots you make during play are forehand and backhand ground strokes. For this reason, the ground strokes should be your basic tools and weapons for winning play.

No two players hit their ground strokes exactly alike. Personal mannerisms, different body builds, differences in temperament—all these determine a player's individual style or form. Some players hit with a loose wrist; others, with a firm wrist. Some use a high loop on the backswing; others, a shallow loop. Some hit the ball relatively flat; others, with topspin. Variations are obvious in practically *all* phases of the strokes, some equally good as others.

Whatever style or form you use can be improved upon. If you are unhappy about your present strokes and want to change them for the better, the tips suggested here might be helpful to you.

Forehand

Backhand

The grip most good players use when making a forehand drive is one in which the palm of the hand is almost behind the racket handle when the racket is edge-down. It's almost as if they were shaking hands with the handle.

Here are some checkpoints that will help you get the proper grip: With the racket face edge-down (like a coin standing on its edge), shake hands with the handle so that:

1. The "V" formed by your thumb and first finger is directly on top of the handle.
2. The soft pads of flesh at the end of your last three fingers are on the wide, vertical plane of the handle (the fingernails of these fingers are facing the net).
3. Your first finger is spread slightly from the other fingers to form a short "trigger finger."
4. Your thumb is between the first finger and the middle finger, resting against the side of the middle finger.

GROUND
STROKES

2

The Ready Position: Stand Like a Baseball Player

When waiting for the ball to be hit to you either when returning a serve or during a rally, stand like a baseball fielder who is waiting for a batter to hit the ball. Face the net, with your feet spread about shoulder-width apart, your weight on the balls of your feet, and your body crouched a little but with your back fairly straight. Bend your knees so that you feel loose and bouncy, ready to move quickly in any direction.

Hold the racket in front of your body at waist height and pointing toward the left net post. From there you'll be ready to move it either to your left or right for either a backhand or a forehand.

Sink down by bending your knees just before your opponent hits the ball, then straighten your knees to push off in the direction you want to go as soon as you see the ball come off your opponent's racket.

GROUND STROKES

Whenever possible, play your ground strokes from a sideways hitting position. Stand like a right-handed batter to hit a forehand; like a left-handed batter to hit a backhand.

The sideways stance makes it easier for you to step toward the ball and to shift your weight forward just before you start your forward swing. In this way you add power as well as control of direction to your shots.

If you face the net as you swing, your hitting arm has a tendency to swing around to the side rather than forward in the direction you are hitting; it tends to swing to the left when you are hitting a forehand and to the right when you are hitting a backhand. You will have a tendency to hit the ball to the side if you hit from the net-facing position and you'll have difficulty hitting where you want to.

3

Stand Sideways

4

Use a Candy-Cane Swing

A simple and effective way to visualize your forehand swing is to think of swinging in the shape of a candy cane that has a long tail. Pretend the candy cane is directly in front of you, lying on its back in midair, with its tail pointed slightly upward toward the net.

As you begin your backswing from the hitting position, swing the racket up, back, and down in the shape of the hook on the candy cane, then swing it forward and gradually upward in the shape of the long tail of the cane. This will produce a slightly looped backswing and a l-o-n-g, slightly rising forward swing and follow-through. Your backswing will actually go around to the right a bit and your follow-through will go to the left, but concentrate on the candy-cane shape and you'll make a pretty good swing.

You can get the same effect by swinging in the shape of a letter "J" that has a long tail. This, too, will produce a slightly looped backswing and a long, rising forward swing and follow-through.

Here's a concept that will help you shape your forehand ground stroke. Stand in the sideways hitting position and pretend a person of average height is standing behind your right shoulder and that a giant 12 feet tall is standing behind your left shoulder. Pretend, too, that each has his hand extended at *his* waist level as if to shake hands with you.

Now swing your racket back, up, then down to loop it over and under the extended hand behind your right hip. Without pausing, swing the racket forward and gradually upward at the ball. Hit the ball, then continue to swing forward and upward until your racket head is "shaking hands with the giant" who is standing to your left.

5

Loop, Then Shake Hands with a Giant

6

Swing from Wall to Wall —Forehand

You can learn the feel of a good forehand swing by practicing the swing while standing with your back to a wall or fence. Stand about one foot from the wall, then swing your racket back until the tip of it barely touches the wall. You'll have to keep your wrist firm to keep the racket from banging against the wall as you swing it back.

When you have completed the backswing, step toward an imaginary ball, shift your weight forward, and make the forward swing. Swing the racket forward and slightly upward, stopping it as its tip barely touches the wall to the left. Here, too, you'll have to have a firm grip and a firm wrist to keep the racket from banging against the wall.

Wall-to-wall swing practice will teach you to control your racket during the swing and acquaint you with the feel of a good, compact, controlled swing.

Visualizing the forehand swing being made over the numerals on a flat-sided clock face will help you learn a good swing. Pretend you are standing on the center of a huge flat-sided clock painted on the court, with the number 12 on the clock being toward the net and number 6 away from the net. Stand sideways, facing number 3, and swing the racket until it is over number 7. Then swing it forward, flattening the arc through the number 3 area, and then upward to the left, stopping it over number 11. The complete swing is from 7 to 11; think about "craps" (7, 11) and you'll remember to make a good swing.

Use the clock face, too, for the backhand swing. Face number 9 on the clock and swing from 5 to 1 or from 4 to 2. Be sure to flatten the arc through the number 9 area. To remind yourself of the backhand swing, think about the word "fortitude" ("four-to-two").

7

Swing from 7 to 11

Forehand

Backhand

8

Bend in the Back, Straight in the Front

For good control on your forehand ground stroke—and for adequate power—bend your hitting arm slightly at its farthest back position during your backswing. Your arm should be neither very close to your body nor straight and stiff away from your body; a slight bend in the elbow is ideal.

You can get the feel of the proper degree of bend in the elbow by pretending you are holding a tennis ball against your side with your elbow.

During the forward swing extend your arm gradually so that at the moment of ball contact it is straight but not stiff. And, at the end of the swing, your arm may be even straighter (but still not stiff).

Practice the swing by actually pressing a ball against your side. The ball will fall to the ground as you swing the racket forward, but you will be learning the proper position of the arm during the backswing. Once you've learned to feel this position, you'll have no trouble using it in your stroke in actual play.

Correct

Elbow too far

Elbow too close

GROUND
STROKES

Where the ball goes when you hit it depends more on where your racket is facing than on any other feature of your swing. You can control the direction the racket faces by making slight adjustments at your wrist joint.

Fix your wrist in what is known as the laid-back position, with the back of your hand at an angle with your forearm rather than in line with it. As you start your swing, lay your wrist back as much as is necessary to make your racket face your intended target. Keep it that way throughout the contact area and you are more likely to hit toward the target than when you use a wristy swing.

While keeping your wrist laid back during the forward swing, move your racket along a line toward the target—along the intended line of flight of the ball—as it passes through the hitting area. By doing so, you can lengthen your hitting area and not have to time your swing very precisely; you can meet the ball at any of several points along the line and still hit with reasonable accuracy. If, on the other hand, your racket travels in an arc and barely moves along the line of the ball, it will be in the proper hitting position—square to the line—for only an instant. At every other instant it will be angled to either the right or left of the line. You will then have to hit the ball at only that one instant to hit accurately.

Lay Your Wrist Back When Hitting Forehand

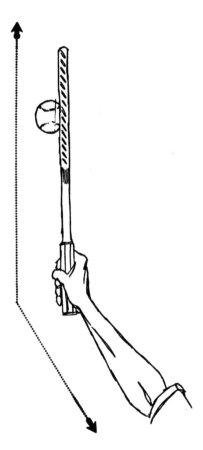

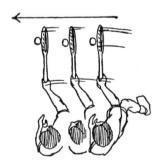

10

Develop the Feel of the Laid-Back Wrist

A slightly laid-back wrist permits you to mistime your swing slightly and still hit reasonably accurately.

To develop the feel of the laid-back wrist, stand in the hitting position alongside the net and press your racket face against the net. Bend your wrist back to keep your racket handle and the racket face parallel to the net. Now draw your racket back away from the net, keeping your wrist in the laid-back position, then swing the racket forward at the net several times, trying to make solid contact with the net with your racket face. Try to whack the net with the racket face as though you were beating a rug.

During actual play, your wrist should look and feel as it does during this exercise. In play, however, the oncoming ball will not stop your racket as the net does and you can follow through. The force of your swing and your arm and body action toward the net will make your racket move progressively ahead of your wrist after ball contact. But at the critical moment, when the racket and ball meet, your wrist should be firm in a laid-back position.

GROUND STROKES

To hit with power on the backhand, you must use a grip that places your palm almost on top of the handle. To get this grip, hold the racket at its throat with your left hand and hold it in front of you in edge-down position. Then grasp the handle with your hitting hand so that:

1. The "V" formed between your thumb and first finger is on the top left narrow plane of the handle.
2. The fleshy ends of your last three fingers are on the bottom left plane of the handle.
3. The first knuckle is almost on top of the handle.
4. The first finger is spread slightly away from the middle finger.
5. The thumb is wrapped around the handle and rests against the side of the middle finger, or, if you prefer, the thumb is slanted diagonally across the back of the handle.

11

The Backhand Grip: Palm on Top

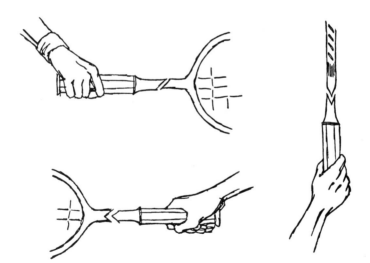

12

Swing from Wall to Wall —Backhand

Use the wall-to-wall concept to learn a good backhand swing. Stand with your back to a wall and about one foot from the wall. Swing your racket back until the tip of it barely touches the wall, keeping your wrist firm so that the racket does not bang against the wall. Step toward an imaginary ball, shift your weight to your front foot, and swing your racket forward at the imaginary ball. Swing your racket forward and to your right a bit, controlling it as you do so your *hand* rather than the tip of the racket touches the wall. You'll have to keep your grip firm and your wrist firm so that neither your hand nor the racket bangs against the wall; your hand should barely touch the wall at the completion of the swing.

Wall-to-wall swing practice will teach you to control your swing so that you will not make the common mistake of overswinging or of flipping your wrist during the stroke.

The backhand swing is very much like the motion you would use to fling a frisbee. Standing sideways like a left-handed baseball batter, turning your upper body so that the back of the right shoulder faces the target, swinging your hand back so that it is very close to your left hip, and stepping toward the target with the front foot—these are all components of both a backhand frisbee toss and a backhand swing. The motions are similar, but not identical.

The important differences between the two are these: You use a lot of wrist-flipping action in flinging a frisbee, and you snap your elbow; whereas in hitting backhand you should keep your wrist very firm and not snap your elbow during the swing. If you want to think about "flinging" at all during a backhand swing, think about flinging from the shoulder.

To hit a backhand, pretend you are trying to fling a frisbee over the far fence, but fling from the shoulder and with a firm wrist.

13

Fling a Frisbee to Hit the Backhand

14

Bat Left Handed to Hit a Backhand

Improve your backhand by pretending you are batting left handed as you hit the ball. During your backswing, slide your nonhitting hand down the racket handle and bring it very close to your hitting hand. You will be holding the racket then almost as you would a baseball bat if you were batting left handed.

With your nonhitting hand close to your hitting hand, swing the racket back until the inside of your right wrist touches your left hip. Turn your upper body so that the back of your hitting shoulder faces the ball. With your hands close together and your upper body turned, you'll have the feeling of being coiled up, ready to deliver a smooth, powerful swing at the ball.

GROUND
STROKES

On the backhand, if your elbow is pointing sharply at the ball, you will have a tendency to poke at the ball. The result is likely to be a weak shot.

One way to correct this poking action is to swing while pressing a ball against your stomach with your hitting forearm during the backswing. With your arm close to your body this way, you'll be able to make a more forceful swing at the ball with full shoulder and body action. The result is more likely to be a long, smooth stroke—the kind that is used by most good players.

Practice the swing by actually pressing a ball against your stomach. The ball will fall to the ground as you move your arm away from your body during the forward swing, but you will be learning the feel of the proper position of the arm during the backswing. Once you've learned this feel, you'll have no trouble using it in your stroke in actual play.

15

Swing at the Ball, Don't Poke at It

16

Adjust Your Timing to Place the Backhand Stroke

Place your backhand ground strokes just as you do your forehand strokes: Make adjustments in the timing of your swing to meet the ball early or late in reference to your straight-ahead contact point. Hit early to hit to the right; hit late to hit to the left. Hit from a closed stance whenever possible, with your front foot slightly closer to the left sideline than your rear foot. Keep your shoulders perpendicular to the net at contact, letting your upper body turn to the right only after you have hit the ball.

How much earlier and later you must hit the ball to place it where you want to will vary each time. It will depend on the angle at which the ball comes to you, the speed of the ball, and how much to the left or right you want it to go. Experience will teach you to make the proper adjustments in the timing of your swing.

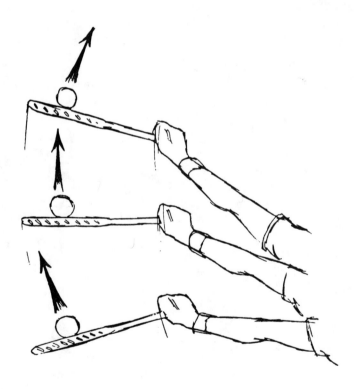

If your backhand grip feels uncomfortable—if it feels weak and awkward as you swing—try using a two-handed backhand. Continue to use your comfortable forehand grip, but reinforce it by using your other hand also. Place your left hand on the racket handle just above your right hand, being careful to align the plane of the palm with the plane of the racket face. Then as you hit the ball your left hand and arm can *push* the racket while your right hand and arm can *pull* it.

You can use either a straight, flat backswing or a slightly looping one. In either case, lower your racket face to just below the level of the ball before you start your forward swing. Then use a powerful body twist with strong arm and shoulder action to pull and push the racket face forward and slightly upward into the ball. Follow through toward your target as far as you can comfortably, then bend your elbows and swing the racket head up and over your right shoulder. At the finish of the swing the upper part of your body should be facing the net.

17

Use Two Hands If Necessary

18

Use a "Two-Forehands" Grip

If the two-handed backhand is your natural shot and you prefer to use it rather than the one-handed shot, be sure the stroke is similar to the one used by the really good two-handed players.

Most of the good two-handers use what can be called a two-forehands grip. To get this grip, place your right hand in the conventional shake-hands-with-the-handle grip as you grasp the racket handle near the butt. Then place your left hand on the handle also, above the right hand but very close to it (the hands should be touching each other or should be nearly touching each other) as if you were shaking hands with the racket with this hand, also.

With your hands in these positions, you can swing at the ball on your left side as though you were using a two-handed, left-handed forehand. Since your left hand will be closest to the racket face, you should feel that it is doing most of the work during the swing; it should provide both power and control. Feel that your right hand is merely reinforcing the left.

For maximum control, keep your *left* wrist in the typical laid-back position as though you were hitting a left-handed forehand. While hitting, move both hands and arms toward your target as far as is comfortable to flatten the arc of your swing. Then bend the elbows so that you finish the swing with the racket head over your right shoulder.

One of the advantages of the two-handed backhand that offsets some of the disadvantages of the shot is the added force you can generate in your swing by using a kind of "couple" action. (The dictionary defines a "couple" as: A pair of equal forces acting in opposite directions and tending to produce rotation.)

As you swing, push against the handle with your right hand while simultaneously pushing in the opposite direction with your left hand. By pushing in opposite directions in this way you can rotate your racket face quickly around your hands and develop a great deal of racket speed. Combine this coupling motion with the conventional body twist and strong shoulder action and you can hit a powerful backhand.

Admittedly, this couple swing is a less-controlled way of hitting the ball than hitting with a laid-back wrist, but when you want to hit with a great deal of power, it may be the best way.

Use a "Couple" Action When Hitting with Two Hands

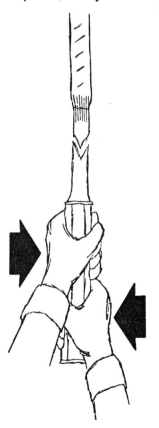

20

Swing Along
a Table Top

If you are dropping your racket head during the backswing when hitting ground strokes, you can correct this by pretending to swing the racket along the top of a slightly inclined waist-high table.

Visualize a table on the court in your hitting zone. As you start your backswing, keep the racket head up so that it is on top of or above the imaginary table. If you're accustomed to dropping your racket head so that it points at the ground as you swing it back, keeping it on the table top might feel strange and uncomfortable for awhile; practice, though, and it will soon become comfortable and automatic.

Use the table-top analogy during your forward swing, too. Swing the racket forward, at the ball, along the inclined table top, then up off the end of the table after you've hit the ball.

To make a smooth, continuous swing on your ground strokes, swing your racket in the shape of an egg. Take your racket *up* and back as the ball approaches you, then gradually loop it, swinging it down and back to just below the level at which you judge the ball will be. Then, without pausing, swing the racket forward and upward toward the ball, making the racket rise gradually so that it hits the ball head-on but with a slightly upward motion.

This continuous egg-shaped motion is better than the go-stop-go motion you would use if you were to swing the racket straight back at waist level. The straight-back swing requires that you stop the racket to make it change directions from backward to forward. Stopping the racket like this could cause you to lay your wrist back too much and destroy the smoothness of your stroke.

21

Use an Egg-Shaped Swing

22

Hit the Ball for a L-O-N-G Time

You can get good control on your ground strokes by swinging "through" the ball and "hitting it for a l-o-n-g time."

To hit for a long time, think of trying to keep the ball on the strings as long as possible. Don't flick or flip your racket at the ball. Instead, swing your racket head directly into the ball and then try to keep the ball on the strings as long as possible, swinging the racket face straight ahead along the line of flight of the ball.

Many good players describe the feeling of hitting for a long time as "trying not to get rid of the ball too quickly."

The hit will feel solid when you hit for a long time and you'll have good control over the direction and flight of the ball. And, as a bonus, you'll hit a "heavy" ball (one that will feel heavy to your opponent when he tries to return it). A heavy ball is more difficult for him to play than an easy, floating ball.

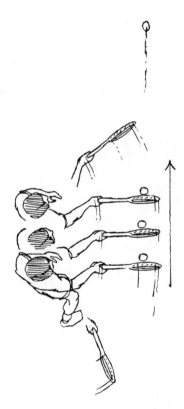

GROUND
STROKES

You can add control to your ground strokes by flattening the arc of your swing so that the racket face moves straight ahead just before, during, and just after ball contact. To flatten the arc, pretend your racket face is a tube as you swing it at the ball. Visualize the ball coming into the front end of the tube, striking the racket strings, and then leaving the tube through the front end, also.

To keep the ball from hitting the sides of the imaginary tube you will have to swing the racket face straight ahead. You will also have to keep the racket face in a standing-on-edge position; if you roll it over or tilt it upward the ball will hit the tube.

The tube concept will also encourage you to follow through straight ahead, adding more control to your shot.

23

"Swing a Tube" to Hit Sound Ground Strokes

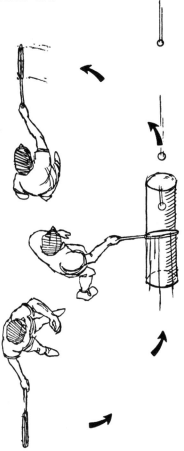

24

Use Your "Gun Barrel" for Control

During the hitting part of your ground strokes (just before, during, and just after ball contact) pretend to swing your racket face forward as though along the line of a gun barrel. The gun barrel is long and straight; think about the hitting zone as being long and straight, also. Swing your racket along the gun barrel and you will guide and steer the ball where you want it to go. The ball will be hit solidly, too, resulting in a "heavy" ball, one that is difficult for your opponent to play.

The gun barrel concept will help you to keep the racket from rolling over or from brushing up, down, or across the ball. It will help you make a good, solid hit.

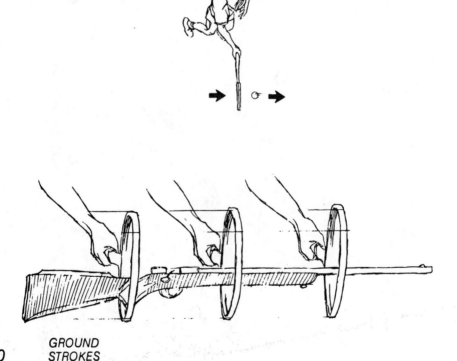

GROUND
        STROKES

A key point in hitting a basic ground stroke, forehand or backhand, is the flattening of the arc of the swinging racket during the forward part of the swing.

The racket face should move straight ahead for an instant before and for an instant after the hit. The entire racket, from the tip of the face to the end of the handle, should be parallel to the net just prior to, during, and just after the hit for a straight-ahead shot. For angle shots, the entire racket should be perpendicular to a line drawn from the target to the racket.

You can swing in this flattened-arc manner if you pretend that you are swinging in the shape of a saucer. Visualize a huge saucer propped up on its edge alongside the court. Swing so that the path of the racket conforms to the shape of the saucer. Avoid a wristy, flippy teacup-shaped swing; instead, use a saucer swing and you'll hit the ball solidly with good control.

25

Use a Saucer Swing Rather Than a Teacup Swing

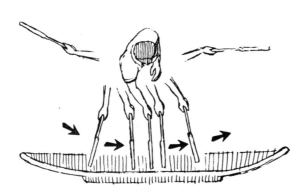

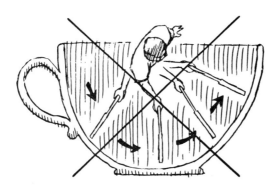

26

Play Your Ground Strokes In Your Strike Zone

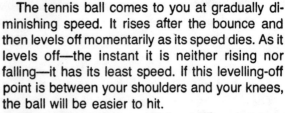

The tennis ball comes to you at gradually diminishing speed. It rises after the bounce and then levels off momentarily as its speed dies. As it levels off—the instant it is neither rising nor falling—it has its least speed. If this levelling-off point is between your shoulders and your knees, the ball will be easier to hit.

Most ground strokes *will* level off somewhere between your shoulders and your knees. Think of this area as your "strike zone" and try to play the ball just as it levels off in this zone.

Pretend that your strike zone is attached to your body. As the ball approaches, move to it (or away from it if it is coming directly at you) so that it enters your strike zone and levels off in the middle of it or nearly so. Move up, back, left, right, or diagonally as necessary.

Hurry to the short balls so that you can play them before they fall down through the strike zone. If you can't get to them in time to play them before they fall through the zone, or if they don't bounce as high as the zone, lower the zone by bending your knees.

Hustle back quickly for deep, high-bouncing balls. If they level off above the strike zone, get back far enough so that you can let them fall down into the zone. They'll be in your strike zone twice, on the way up and on the way down, but play them on the way down and your timing and judgment of them will be easy.

GROUND STROKES

To hit the ball with topspin to make it drop after it crosses the net, the racket head must be moving upward across the back of the ball. This is often described as "brushing the strings up the back of the ball."

An equally effective concept is to imagine that the ball consists of two movable halves. As you hit it, pretend you are trying to move the near half (the half closest to you) upward so that it separates from the far half (the half closest to the net) and slides upward.

To hit with backspin, reverse the procedure: Imagine that you are trying to separate the two halves by making the near side slide downward.

To spin a serve, pretend you are trying to slide the near half of the ball sideward across the far side.

27

Hit Up on the Ball for Topspin

28

Hit the Near or Far Side of the Ball

You can control the direction of your shots by swinging in the direction you are aiming. In addition, however, you must make slight and subtle changes in the angle of the racket face (to the ball) at impact.

To hit cross-court, change the angle so that you *feel* you are hitting the ball a bit on its far side (the side farthest from you). You'll actually be hitting the ball head-on, flush on its center, but you should feel that you are sort of swinging around it to hit it just a bit on its far side.

To hit down the line, swing from inside out somewhat to *feel* that you are hitting the ball a bit on its near side (the side nearest to you). Again, you'll hit the ball head-on, but the feel of hitting it on the near side will help you guide it where you want it to go.

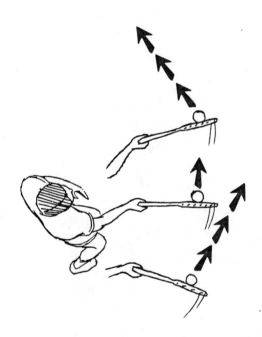

To place the ball when you hit ground strokes you must make subtle changes in your timing and in your wrist-racket angle. Equally important, however, is swinging along the line you want the ball to go.

Imagine that the ball approaches you along a railroad track and that you want to hit it along another railroad track that crosses the first one. When you hit the ball with this track concept in mind, actually try to steer the ball along the track. This will force you to be extremely careful in your follow-through; you'll have to follow through along the track and most likely the ball will go where you want it to.

29

Steer the Ball Along a Railroad Track

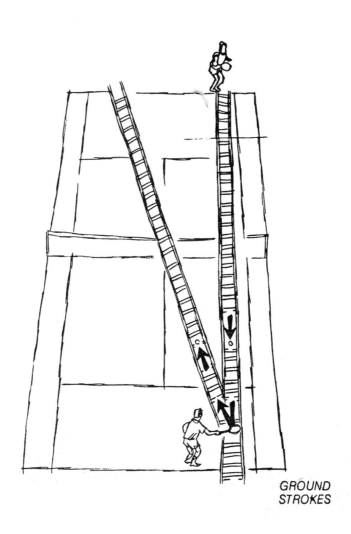

30

Move from
Rail to Rail
to Play Close Balls

When the ball comes directly at you when you are playing in the backcourt, you must move to the side of it quickly in order to stroke it properly.

Visualize this ball coming to you along one rail of a railroad track while you are standing astride that rail. As the ball approaches, quickly move to the other rail, to the side, so you can take a full swing at the ball.

Use the same analogy when running forward to play a short ball. Don't run directly at the ball (to the rail on which it is approaching), but to the side of the ball (to the other rail) so you can play it with a sidearm swing.

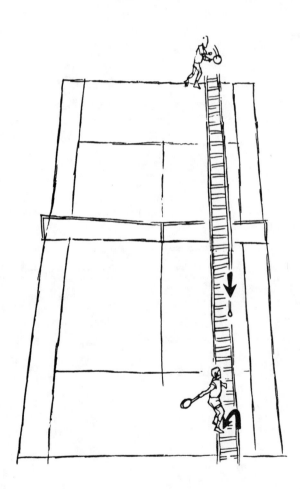

Learn to tailor the length of your backswing to the needs of the situation. Use a long, full swing to hit a ball that is coming at you slowly; the ball has little speed on it and to add speed to your return of it you must first generate good racket speed by using a long, full swing.

Use a short, compact backswing to return a fast ball; you don't have to add speed to this ball, but you do have to time it accurately and hit it solidly. A short, compact backswing will make timing easier than a long swing.

Use a short swing for low shots in midcourt, too, when you have no choice but to hit the ball up and easy, and for scrambling shots when you are merely trying to get the ball back in play.

31

Vary the Length of Your Backswing

32

Move Away from the Ball in the Backcourt

When you are playing from the backcourt in singles you should seldom be exactly in the center of the court directly behind the center mark. The only time you should be there is when your opponent is hitting from the exact middle of his court; at all other times you should be slightly off-center, away from the side the ball is on.

If you have forced your opponent to hit from his forehand corner, you should move a little to the right of your center mark as you await his shot; if you have forced him to hit from his backhand corner, you should move a little to the left of your center mark.

Moving off-center like this—moving away from the side the ball is on—will put you in a good position to cover both a cross-court shot and a down-the-line shot made by him. If, instead of moving to an off-center position, you were to stay in the center of the court, you would have real difficulty getting to a cross-court shot.

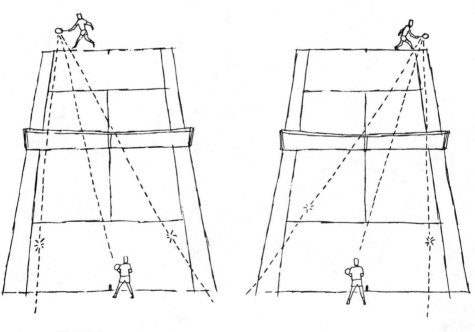

GROUND
STROKES

To hit accurately and consistently, you must be sensitive to the position of your racket during your swing. If, at contact, the hitting surface of the racket is slanted skyward in an open position, the ball will go up; if the hitting surface is slanted downward in a closed position, the ball will go down.

For most ground strokes your racket face should be perpendicular to the ground or very nearly so. One good way to learn the feel of the hand and arm positions that result in a perpendicular racket position is to bounce the ball with the bottom edge of the racket, dribbling the ball much like a basketball player dribbles a basketball.

After several successive bounces (or dribbles), change your vertical swing to a horizontal one and drive the ball toward the net. You will probably hit a line drive typical of most effective ground strokes.

Once you have learned the feel of the perpendicular racket, use this feel to hit your ground strokes as you rally and play.

33

Hit with Your Racket "on Edge"

34

Practice Angled Ground Strokes

During play only occasionally do you hit a ball that comes straight to you from directly in front of you. Most often you play a ball that comes to you from a slight angle, from one corner of the court or the other. Only occasionally, too, do you hit straight ahead; most often you hit an angle shot to one corner or the other.

Practice these angled shots by rallying with a partner, with each of you trying to run the other from corner to corner. When he hits from one corner, aim your return, forehand or backhand, to the opposite corner. Ask him to do the same so that you can practice hitting balls that come to you from both corners of the court.

By rallying this way regularly you'll learn the subtle changes in timing and wrist action necessary to make these angled shots.

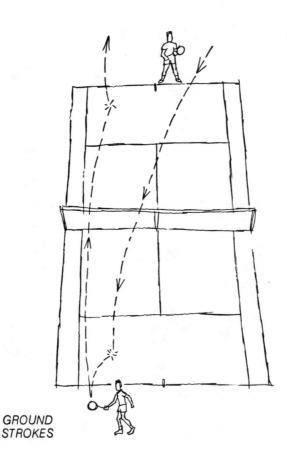

GROUND STROKES

SERVE

Top-ranked players exhibit fewer variations in style and form in their serves than in any other stroke of the game.

Most of the better players use a combination of topspin and sidespin as their basic serve. They vary the spin and speed when they serve, depending upon whether they're making a first or second serve, but they use a spin serve as their basic one.

Imitate these top players; make the spin serve your basic serve, too. Flat serves, twist serves, and extreme-slice serves are advanced serves. They're nice to have in your arsenal but not absolutely necessary for success. Experiment with them, but only after you have developed a safe, reliable spin serve.

Serve

As you take up your position to serve, pretend you are getting ready to throw a ball over the net, and stand like a thrower. Stand so that a line drawn from the toes of your rear foot past the toes of your front foot points toward your target (the service court), and so that your feet are spread apart wide enough to enable you to pass your racket face edgewise between your knees. Point your front foot in the general direction of the right net post and place your rear foot parallel to the baseline.

This thrower's stance will give you a wide, steady base, one from which you are more likely to make a good serve than if you were to stand with your feet close together in a tippy position.

35

Stand Like a Thrower to Serve

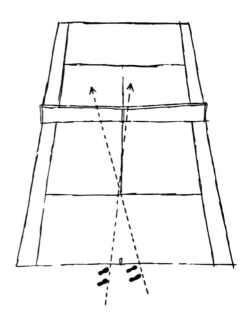

36

Use a Finger Grip When Serving

You must use a lot of wrist and hand action to serve hard; you must fling the racket head at the ball with great force. For this reason most, though not all, hard servers use a backhand grip or an almost-a-backhand grip when serving. With the palm of the hitting hand almost on the top plane of the racket handle, they can whip the racket head up and over at the ball with great speed.

Try a backhand or almost-a-backhand grip to add power to your serve. If you have trouble controlling the serve with these grips, however, use a forehand grip instead, but hold the racket more in the fingers than you would when hitting a forehand ground stroke. This in-the-fingers grip will permit you to put a lot of hand action into the shot without a loss of control.

Unless you are very tall—over six feet—your basic serve should be one that spins slightly. Forget about the flat serve—it's a risky one even for tall players. Spin the ball a bit to make it curve downward into the service court.

To serve a basic spin serve, pretend the ball is a top as you hit it. Toss it up almost directly above the toes of your front foot about as high as you can reach with the top edge of the racket. Then, as you swing at it, keep the top concept in mind and simply "spin the top." You'll have to hit the ball with a very slight left-to-right action to spin it, but your swing should be primarily a forward one.

Experiment a bit. Find out precisely what combination of forward motion and left-to-right motion you must use to serve consistently and with power. When you have found it, use this combination for your basic spin serve.

37

Spin a Top for Your Basic Serve

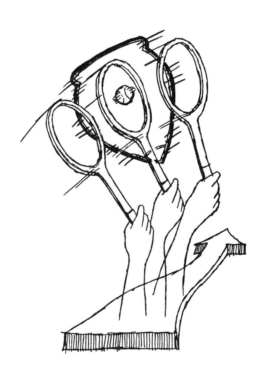

38

Spread Your Wings to Serve

You can smooth out the tricky downward and upward movement of your arms when serving by using the simple concept of "spreading your wings."

As you stand in position to serve, place your hands out in front of you toward the net. Swing them down together to just in front of your left thigh, then pretend to spread your wings by swinging the left arm forward and up (to toss the ball) and the right arm back and up (to cock the racket head up beyond your right shoulder) simultaneously.

Spread your wings several times without tossing the ball until the movement feels comfortable and easy for you, then simply release the ball during the upward movement of your left arm and swing the racket at the ball.

When you are standing in position ready to serve, there are several convenient checkpoints you can use to make a good swing. First, swing your racket head down past your KNEES (swing your tossing arm down toward your left thigh at the same time), then swing it back and up toward the top of the rear FENCE (swing your tossing arm forward and up at the same time). As the tossed ball reaches its peak, swing the racket head down behind your BACK, then swing it forward and up to HIT the ball.

Think "KNEE, FENCE, BACK, and HIT!" (toss and shift your weight on FENCE) and you'll get a pretty good swing at the ball.

39

Knee, Fence, Back, and Hit! To Serve

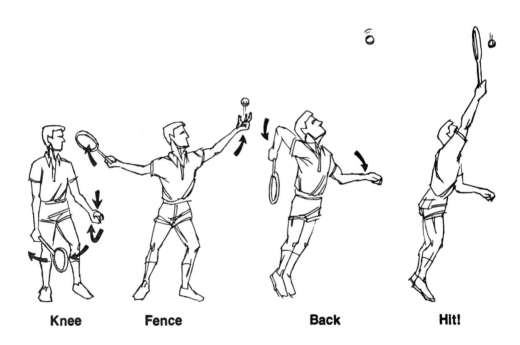

| Knee | Fence | Back | Hit! |

40

Sight, Spread, Scratch, and Hit!

If you feel uncoordinated when you serve, here's a sequence of moves that will smooth out your swing.

In the starting position, SIGHT along your racket face as though you were aiming at a target (the service court to which you are hitting). Then "SPREAD your wings" to swing your arms down together then up simultaneously in opposite directions; move your tossing arm forward and up to toss the ball and move your hitting arm back and up to cock the racket up behind your right shoulder. Then "SCRATCH your back" as you loop the racket head down behind your right shoulder before swinging it up and forward to HIT the ball.

Follow the sequence of SIGHT, SPREAD, SCRATCH, and HIT! and you'll make a well-coordinated swing and a good hit.

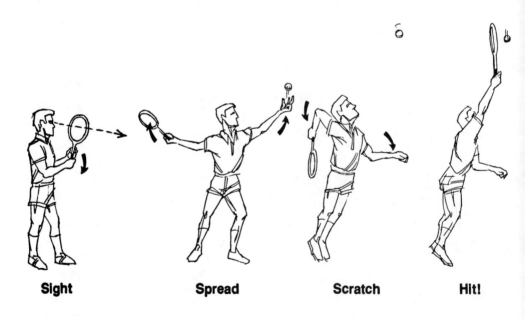

| Sight | Spread | Scratch | Hit! |

Add power to your serve by using a throwing motion when you hit the ball. Swing your hitting arm down and away from the net, then swing it back and up toward the top of the rear fence. Keep your palm down (almost facing the ground) and your elbow up and away from your body as you swing your arm back and up. Your elbow should be about shoulder high. Your shoulders should tilt, however, during the toss-and-backswing part of the swing; your tossing shoulder should rise as you toss, and your hitting shoulder should drop a bit. Your elbow, then, should be about as high as your hitting shoulder, with the upper part of your arm parallel to the ground.

With your elbow up and away from your body and your palm down, you will be in good position to "throw" the racket head at the ball and really add power to your serve. The throwing motion, however, should be like the one an outfielder in baseball would use if he were to throw the ball from the outfield to home base—it should be an upward one rather than a downward one or parallel-to-the-ground one a baseball pitcher would use.

41

Throw Like an Outfielder When Serving

42

Toss from a Tripod

To serve consistently, you must toss accurately. If you toss to a different place every time you serve, you must use a different swing every time. As a result, you'll have trouble "grooving" your swing.

Serve by holding two balls in your tossing hand. Place one ball in the tripod formed by your thumb and first two fingers, letting it rest on the inside edge of your curled-under ring finger; your little finger will naturally curl under, also. Place the second ball in the palm of your hand, below the first ball, holding it in place with pressure from the last two fingers.

To toss the ball (the first ball), simply launch it from the tripod by opening your fingers during the upward motion of your tossing arm.

To toss the second ball after a fault, simply move this ball up to the tripod and launch it as you did the first ball.

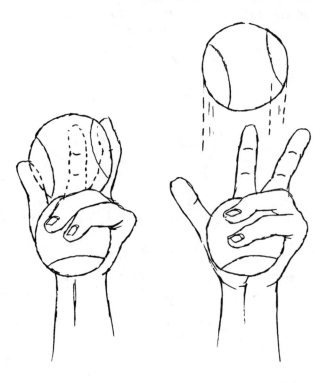

For a consistent toss when serving, pretend you are pushing the ball upward as though it would pass through a vertical tube suspended above you in midair. To toss through the tube, you wouldn't flip or fling the ball up as if it were a hot potato; most likely you would swing your tossing hand up carefully to bring it (and the ball) close to the opening in the tube. Then you would merely "push" the ball into the opening, releasing it from your fingers as your hand got close to the end of the tube.

Don't throw, flip, or fling the ball. Push it up carefully—push it through a tube—and you'll make accurate tosses and develop a steady, consistent serve.

43

Push the Ball Up Through a Tube

44

Toss in Line with a Fence Post

Occasionally during play your toss will go awry and you'll not be able to toss where you want to consistently. An erratic toss, of course, will result in an erratic, inconsistent serve. When your serve becomes shaky and you suspect your toss is at fault, there is a corrective measure you can use.

As you take your serving position, look at the far fence and pick out a fence post that is in line with where you want your toss to be. Then, as you toss, be conscious of the post (you can see it in the background of your vision) and bring your tossing arm up in line with the post. Using the post as a guide will often immediately correct a faulty toss.

The toss is a critical part of the serve. To serve effectively and consistently you must toss to the same spot—or to nearly the same spot—each time you serve. You must toss in the plane in which you intend to swing so you can groove your swing in that plane. If you toss to different places each time and then swing wherever you toss, you'll never groove your swing; you'll have to learn several different swings to accommodate several different tosses.

If your toss is erratic, one way to improve it is to watch yourself make it. Look at your tossing hand as you serve and follow it with your eyes as you move it down and then up to toss. Then watch the ball as it moves upward out of your hand.

Don't look upward to where you intend to place the ball. Instead, watch yourself (your hand) place it there. Regular practice in watching your tossing hand will improve the consistency of your toss.

45

Watch Your Toss as You Serve

46

Use a Delayed Toss

If you have trouble coordinating your arm movements when serving, use a delayed toss serve for a while: Move one arm first (the hitting arm), then move the other arm (the tossing arm).

Start in the normal serving position. Move your hitting arm down and back to swing your racket past your knees then up toward the top of the rear fence. *Stop* in this position. Now move your tossing arm down and up to toss the ball. When the ball reaches the peak of the toss, swing your racket through the conventional back-scratching position then up and forward to hit the ball. Be sure to stop the racket when it is cocked up behind your right shoulder and *not* when it is in the back-scratching position; the racket should *move through* the back-scratch position and not stop there.

Delaying your toss in this manner is a good way to control the serve *if* you have trouble trying to move both arms at the same time. Try it for a while, and eventually you will be able to move both arms simultaneously.

A forward shift of weight is one of several sources of power used in serving. Most good players either shift and toss at the same time, or toss then shift; few, if any, shift and then toss, yet this is what most inexperienced players do. Because they shift too soon, they swing from a wobbly, precarious position, and they can't get much power in their serves.

For an inexperienced player, probably the most efficient way to use the shift of weight as a source of power is to toss then shift. If your serve lacks power, perhaps you can add power by trying this method. Lean back, placing your weight on your rear foot, toss the ball and let it hang in the air momentarily while you get it in your sights, *then* shift your weight forward and hit the ball. You'll have good balance this way because you'll be swinging on a solid, wide base, and you'll be getting your weight into the shot at the proper moment.

47

Toss Before You Shift When Serving

48

Use a Long Grip When Serving

For more power when serving, try the butt-in-the-palm grip. Instead of letting the butt of your handle stick out below your hand as you usually do, move your hand down toward the end of the handle so that your palm covers the butt. This will make a longer lever of the racket, and if you can manage to swing it with as much force as you normally do, you'll have more racket speed at impact. The result will be a faster serve.

In addition, the longer grip usually engenders more wrist action at contact, and this too adds power to the serve.

But if you have trouble controlling your serves with the longer grip, revert to your normal grip and serve in your usual manner, especially on the second serve. You can't risk missing those, so serve in the safest way possible. Use the long grip in practice, however, and you'll learn to serve consistently with it.

To add speed to your serve, try jumping as you hit the ball. Most of the top players jump a bit, either deliberately or unconsciously.

Try jumping in two different ways: (1) jump from the front foot to the rear foot, swinging your rear foot over and across the baseline so that you land on this foot inside the baseline; (2) jump from the front foot to the front foot, landing on this foot just behind the baseline.

The first method is most common. It adds power to the hit and gives you an early start on the way to the net. The second method could add power, also, but it delays your advance momentarily.

Many good players use the first method on the first serve (for power) and the second method on the second serve (for spin and control). Try both methods and see which works best for you.

49

Jump to Add Power to Your Serve

50

Full Speed Just After the Hit

If you have a sound serve swing but can't seem to serve as hard as you'd like to, perhaps you're not swinging as hard as you can or as hard as you think you are. You might be fearful of missing the serve and might be slowing down your swing subconsciously just before your racket meets the ball, so that your racket head is decelerating rather than accelerating at impact.

To develop maximum racket speed at impact, swing hard but feel that you are developing maximum speed *just after* impact. This will ensure that your racket is not decelerating at impact, and you'll get full power in your serve.

Improve the timing of your serve by taking your time as you swing. Make a momentary balance-gathering pause just before starting the forward and upward swing at the ball and you'll be able to hit the ball cleanly and squarely.

Start your backswing slowly. When you reach the outstretched-arms position, your left arm will be in a Statue of Liberty position, the upper part of your hitting arm will be parallel to the ground, and your racket will be cocked upward in back of your right shoulder. Your entire body will be in a tilted "Y" position.

This is the time to slow down; feel that you actually pause momentarily as you wait for the ball to start falling. You'll have good balance and you'll be able to see the ball clearly—it will seem to be hanging in the air just waiting to be hit—and you'll be able to "powder it."

51

Pause Momentarily as You Serve

52

Change Your Toss to Correct Your Serve

If your serves are going long consistently, it could be because (1) you're not tossing the ball far enough forward, or (2) you're leading with your wrist at impact. In either case, you would be hitting the underside of the ball (the bottom half); if there were a face on the ball, you would be hitting the ball on its chin.

To correct this, toss farther forward and flip your racket head *up* and *over* to hit the ball on its forehead rather than on its chin.

Netted serves are usually caused by hitting the ball too high on its forehead (almost on top of its head) as a result of tossing too far forward and of swinging down at the ball. Correct these netted serves by tossing the ball back farther and by swinging *up* and *out* at it so that you hit it more on its nose.

If your normal toss places the ball directly in line with the sun so that you are blinded momentarily when serving, make a slight change in your toss. Try a few experimental tosses, tossing to the left and to the right of where you normally toss. Most likely you'll find that one of these tosses will place the ball out of the line of the sun and that you'll see the ball clearly and not be blinded by the sun.

As you change your toss, you'll have to change your swing a bit. Your serve will be different from your normal one and perhaps a little less effective than your normal one, but at least you'll be able to avoid double faults.

53

Change Your Toss When Serving In the Sun

54

Change Your Stance When Serving In the Sun

Another way of adjusting your serve when serving in the sun is to change your stance. Stand either more or less sideways than you normally do, then toss the ball to the same spot you normally do; the ball will be in a different spot relative to the sun and you'll be able to see it as you swing at it.

This new stance will force you to change your swing pattern slightly, so don't expect to serve as well as you do under ideal conditions. At least, however, you should have clear sighting at the ball and you should be able to avoid double faulting.

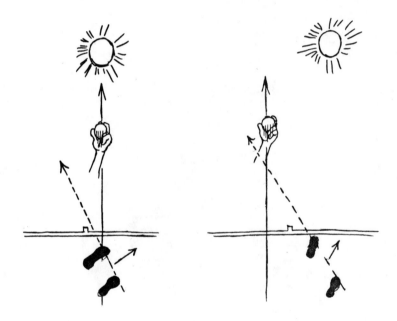

Rarely, if ever, should you hit a perfectly flat serve. Most often you should hit with enough spin to make the ball hook or bend after it crosses the net.

To hit with spin, don't hit the ball head-on with a flat racket face; hit it a slight glancing blow. Swing so that your racket face moves slightly up and across the intended line of flight of the ball; pretend there is a face on the ball and that your racket is hitting the ball on its nose but moving toward its left eye.

With practice you can learn to vary the degree to which you swing up and across the ball and thus vary the degree of spin on the ball. You'll be able to control the hook or bend of the ball.

55

Hook or Bend Your Serves

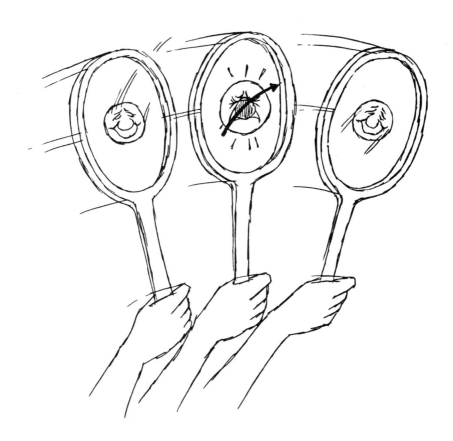

56

Hit from 7 to 2 for a Twist

One of the most difficult serves to return is a high-bouncing twist to the backhand. The ball kicks up and to the left of the receiver as it bounces, forcing him to play a difficult high backhand.

To serve a twist, toss the ball to the left of where you normally toss it for your basic slice serve. During the forward swing, bend your back to the left and swing your hitting arm, with a bent elbow, so that you swing your racket face up and across the ball, from the left to right. Pretend there is a clock face on the ball and swing from 7 to 2 on the clock face. You'll actually hit the ball where the hands connect, but the racket face will be moving across the ball, hitting it a glancing blow. Try to create a "swishing" sound as you whisk the strings up and across the ball from 7 to 2 on the imaginary clock face.

If the full-swing twist serve is too strenuous for you—if it puts too much strain on your back and stomach muscles—you can modify the swing somewhat and still serve an effective twist.

Dispense with the strenuous back-arching motion used in the full swing. Simply toss the ball slightly to the left of your head, then sort of reach around your head as you swing at the ball. Bend your hitting arm as you whisk the strings across the ball in a forward and slightly upward direction, using only as much vigorous arm and wrist action as is comfortable for you.

You'll not get as much spin on the ball with this modified swing, but you'll get sufficient spin to make a fairly effective serve.

57

Serve a Modified Twist

58

Increase Your Margin for Error When Serving

We all like to hit flat, spectacular, cannonball serves, but consider this: A player who is 6 feet tall reaches about 3 feet above his head to contact the ball when serving. If he hits the ball flat, so that it has very little or no spin on it, and hard enough so that the downward pull of gravity has no effect on it, the ball would have to clear the net by *not more than 6 inches* to land within the service line; any ball clearing the net by more than 6 inches would land outside the service court. This 6-inch margin for error is much too little for all but the best of players.

You can increase your margin for error by spinning your serve. Spin it so that it curves and hooks downward after crossing the net; you'll have a bigger margin of safety and you'll get a lot more serves in.

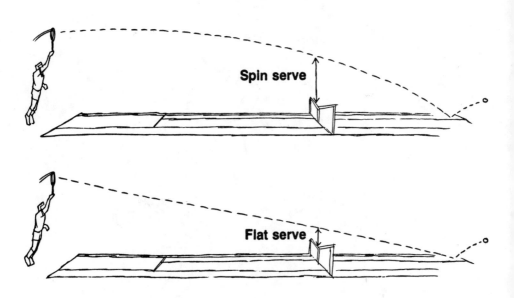

Spin serve

Flat serve

Stop-action pictures of hard-hit serves show clearly that shortly after ball contact the left edge of the racket is closer to the net than the right edge. What happens is that the hitting forearm turns inward (counterclockwise) momentarily as the racket is swung forward toward the net. Experts in the field of body mechanics tell us that the arm assumes a position of comfort to avoid putting strain on the elbow.

This inward turning of the arm is brief and barely perceptible; the right edge of the racket quickly resumes its lead as the stroke is completed.

You need not think about turning your forearm inward when you serve hard; it's a natural movement, so just let it happen. Don't, however, fight it by trying to carve the ball by curving your racket face around the right side of the ball.

59

Don't Carve Your Serves

Don't curve your racket around the ball

60

**Stand Near
the Center Mark
When Serving**

When serving from the right side in singles, stand just to the right of the center mark. This will enable you to serve to the receiver's backhand most easily (your serve will pass over the lowest part of the net on the way to his backhand side); it will also enable you to play many of his returns with your strong forehand (if he returns down the middle, you can run around your backhand to play a forehand).

In the left court, stand about six feet to the left of the center mark. From here, too, you'll be able to serve to the receiver's backhand fairly easily, and, except for returns sharply angled to your left, you will be able to run around your backhand and play the ball with your strong forehand.

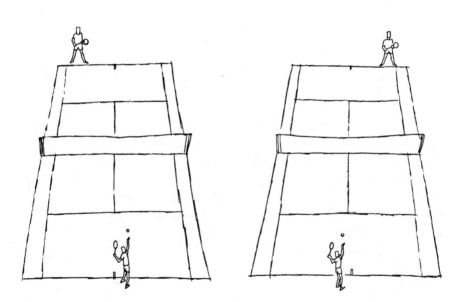

Vary your procedure and rhythm when serving to keep your opponent off-balance; don't let him get grooved to your rhythm.

Vary the number of times you bounce the ball when you stand in the serving position. Bounce it once sometimes, bounce it twice sometimes, bounce it three or four times sometimes, and sometimes don't bounce it at all. Each time you serve he'll begin to wonder how many times you're going to bounce the ball. His concentration on returning the ball will be affected somewhat and he'll probably miss a lot more returns than if you were to follow the same procedure or routine every time.

There's nothing contrary to the rules in doing this; it's a perfectly legitimate way to use subtle tactics during play.

61

Vary Your Procedure When Serving

62

Vary Your Tactics When Serving

When serving, you have several choices of placement that can increase the effectiveness of your serve.

A wide serve toward a sideline may force your opponent out of position, thus giving you an opening for your next shot. When serving wide to your opponent's forehand in the right court, for example, you will be opening his backhand side for your next shot.

But your wide serve might give him the chance to move you out of position, too; he might return the ball wide to your forehand side, forcing you to go wide, thus opening your backhand side for *his* next shot. At times, then, it might be best to serve down the middle to reduce his angles, thus making his returns less effective.

Consider the advantages of each placement. It might be best for you to serve wide in one court and down the middle in the other. Serving to make him weak in position (by forcing him wide) might outweigh the disadvantage of serving to his stronger stroke. Similarly, serving to his stronger stroke might be more advantageous than serving wide to his weaker stroke and thereby giving him good angles for his returns.

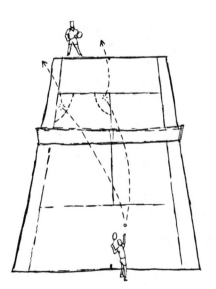 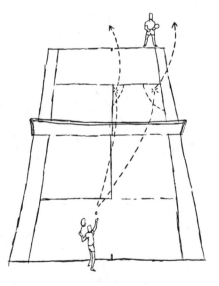

When you serve wide to your opponent to make him return the ball from his alley, get ready for his return by making a ready-hop just as he winds up to hit the ball. If you stay back near the baseline after you serve, you should make this ready-hop a few feet to the side of the center mark, on the side of the center mark *away* from the ball.

When you serve wide and follow your serve to the net, again make your ready-hop just as he winds up to hit the ball. But in this instance you should be in the forecourt area, and when you make the ready-hop you should be to the side of the center line *toward* the ball.

In both instances—in the backcourt and at the net—you should be off-center a bit. Though this off-center distance is small—it should never be more than two or three feet—it often makes the difference between getting to your opponent's return and not getting to it.

63

Be Off-Center After You Serve

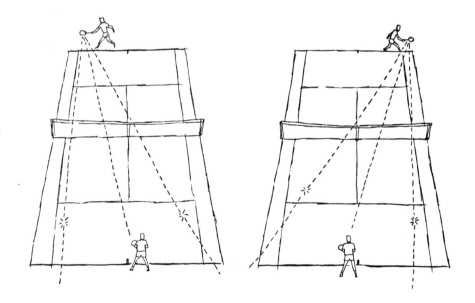

64

Follow Your Serve to the Net

If you serve well enough to prevent your opponent from making an aggressive return, follow your serve to the net. You will then be in position to take advantage of a weak service return.

When you go to the net, stop running and make a ready-hop just as your opponent winds up to make his return. You want to get as close to the net position as you can, but, even more importantly, you want to be ready to move to the ball for the next shot. Adjust the number of steps you take as you go up according to the amount of time you have between your serve and his windup.

After a hard, fast serve, you might have time for only two or three steps and you will have to make your ready-hop in no man's land, but you can risk being caught there after a hard serve. Chances are your opponent's return will be weak, and you'll be able to deal with it effectively.

A slower serve might allow time for four or five steps and let you get closer to an ideal volleying position. Here, too, make a ready-hop just as your opponent starts his windup.

In either case—whether in no man's land or closer to the ideal volleying position—move forward to the ideal volleying position after you make your first volley.

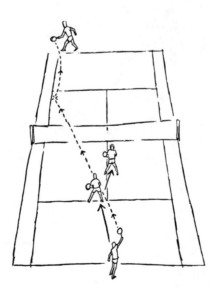

One of the popular axioms of tennis is that you are only as good as your second serve. If you have a hard, fast first serve but miss a large percentage of them, you'll be serving a lot of second serves during a match. If these second serves are soft, easy-to-handle ones, your opponent is sure to take advantage of them by hitting attacking returns.

You might serve more effectively by discarding your normal hard first serve for a slower first serve, even if it means giving up the chance of acing your opponent. Serve more softly than you normally do but still hard enough to prevent him from attacking with his return. You are then likely to have an easier shot for your first ground stroke, and if your tactics and strokes are up to par, you should be able to control the rally that follows.

65

Serve Well Enough to Control the Rally

66

Improve
Your Second Serve
by Playing
One-Serve Tennis

If your second serve is shaky and you serve a lot of double faults, practice this serve. If you serve a mild twist or spin serve when serving the second ball, serve this way when you practice. But, to make your practice sessions more realistic and gamelike, agree with a practice partner that you will have only one serve as you and he play. Play, then, and pretend each time you serve that you have already missed your first serve and you are serving the second ball.

By limiting yourself to only one serve when you play during your practice sessions, you will be putting pressure on yourself when you serve. This will be very much like the situation during actual play when you have missed the first serve.

Regular practice playing one-serve tennis will help you get over the fear of missing your second serve in actual play. You'll convince yourself that you *can* get that second serve in, and you will start getting a lot of them in during play.

Most of us want to abide by the rules, even in friendly club play. Yet we frequently break a rule without realizing it, though usually not intentionally: We step on the baseline or across it into the court before we strike the ball when serving.

To find out if *you* are foot-faulting when you serve, place a yardstick or similar stick on the baseline in front of you and serve a few balls. If you touch the stick or knock it off the line, you are obviously foot-faulting. You have probably moved your front foot during the swing without realizing it.

To correct this, practice serving with the stick on the line. You will quickly learn to keep your front foot steady or to adjust your serving motion in some other way to keep from foot-faulting.

67

Correct Your Foot Faults

68

Practice Serving with a Covered Racket

Wrist action should be a major source of power in your serve. You should whip your racket head up and into the ball as fast as you can, flipping your wrist at the last split second before ball contact.

A good way to add wrist action to your serve is to practice serving against a fence or wall with a cover on your racket head. The standard racket head cover is ideal for this. As you hit the ball toward the fence, you'll feel the added air resistance of the cover and you'll feel the wrist action you'll need to overcome this resistance.

When you remove the cover after this practice, your racket will feel very light. And, if you use the same wrist action when serving, you'll be swinging your racket faster and be serving much harder.

Regular practice in covered-racket serving will help you develop a strong serve. Be sure you practice by serving against a fence, however. If you practice by serving on the court, trying to get the serve in the proper service court, you'll have to alter your normal swing pattern too much to get the ball in. Use the covered racket only to develop wrist action.

You can practice your serve at home by actually hitting a soft, simulated tennis ball. Such balls are available commercially (they're made of sponge rubber), but you can use a homemade one equally well.

To make such a ball, cut the foot section off an old sock and stuff it with newspaper. Then roll this foot section into a ball about the size of a tennis ball and bind it with rubber bands or cellophane tape. You can toss this soft ball as you would a regular ball and practice your serve with it by serving against the side of your house or against your garage door.

Regular practice with this simulated ball will help you develop a consistent toss and a consistent serve.

69

Practice Your Serve at Home

VOLLEYS

In high-level play, the volleys are extremely important strokes; together with the big serve, they form the basis for the big game now used by most top players. Even if you are a low-level player, however, there will be occasions when you will be forced to volley during play, so you must learn to make these shots.

The ability to volley well is a prime necessity if you have any aspirations to advance beyond the intermediate level of play. If you play exclusively from the backcourt, you might enjoy some success, but an all-court game consisting of sound ground strokes, an effective serve, *and* forcing, penetrating volleys should be your objective. Only with such an all-court game can you be considered a truly well-rounded player ready for any emergency.

Forehand

Backhand

Remember the childhood game of patty-cake in which one child patted his hand against another child's hand? This simple concept will help you learn the rudiments of a good forehand volley.

As the ball approaches you when you are at the net, step toward it with your left foot and raise your racket head up and behind the point in the air where you judge the ball will be when it reaches you. Then, when the ball arrives, jab the racket face at it in patty-cake fashion, trying to hit it squarely in the center of the racket face. Don't swing at the ball, merely patty-cake it and you'll make a good, firm volley.

70

Patty-Cake
Your Forehand Volley

71

Beat a Rug to Volley

The normal volley should be made with a short, firm, compact jabbing motion; not much backswing or forward swing is necessary.

If you are overswinging on your volleys, the concept of "beating a rug" with your racket head will help you make a more effective short, crisp swing.

Pretend that a rug is hanging over a clothesline and is suspended downward in a vertical plane that passes through the point at which you want to hit the ball, and that you are standing just to the side of and in front of the rug. As the ball meets the plane of the rug, beat the rug with your racket head, pretending to slap it with the flattened-out racket face. The short, firm swing you'll use will result in a firm, controlled volley.

You must have a firm grip on the racket to volley well, and, on most high volleys, you need to use only a short jabbing motion, jabbing the racket face at the ball.

You can get the feel of the stroke by pretending one end of a long rubber band is attached to the throat of your racket as you make the volley and that someone is holding the other end of the rubber band. Jab the racket face at the ball, s-t-r-e-t-c-h-i-n-g the imaginary rubber band as you hit the ball.

You can use the same concept for low volleys; you must jab forward and downward on these, however, to put some backspin on the ball, and you must jab much more easily.

72

Stretch a Rubber Band When You Volley

73

Block, Jab, or Drive Your Volleys

Learn to vary the stroke you use when volleying. If a ball is hit to you very hard, all you need to do—and all you'll have time to do—is merely block the ball back. With a firm grip and wrist, simply place the racket head in front of the ball and let the ball rebound off it. You don't have to add speed to the ball; all you have to do is control the direction of its rebound off the racket.

You will have to add speed to slow balls that are driven at you. Use a jabbing motion to do so, jabbing the racket head at the ball. Play the low volleys carefully, jabbing easily forward *and* downward to underspin them.

If you get a slow, lazy floater, use a short-swing drive to add a lot of speed to your shot. Merely blocking or jabbing the ball will result in too little speed on your shot, so drive-volley the ball by using a short, compact drive-swing.

Think of using as much swing as you have time for; block, jab, or drive-volley depending upon the time you have.

A good volleyer lets only very good drives go past him without trying for them. He tries for every ball, almost as if he were a goalkeeper in soccer or hockey.

Try this concept when you are at the net: Pretend *you* are tending goal and that any ball that gets past you is scored against you. Remember that your opponent will *try* to hit the ball past you, so be prepared to move left or right to protect your goal. When waiting for your opponent to hit, bend your knees, crouch a little, and be prepared mentally and physically to prevent the ball from getting past you. You won't need to use a big swing to prevent a goal from being scored; merely move quickly and get your racket head in front of the ball.

74

Play Goal to Learn to Volley

75

Keep the Racket Looking Almost Straight Ahead

Use a short, compact jabbing or punching motion when volleying, with a short backswing and practically no follow-through. Visualize the racket face as looking straight ahead at impact and try to keep it that way after the hit. You won't be able to keep it looking exactly straight ahead; the forward momentum of your arm and the racket will cause the racket face to move forward somewhat, but try to curtail this movement.

Keep your wrist firm—don't change your wrist angle—during the stroke. This will keep the racket from flipping at the ball. If the racket does flip, the racket face will be looking down after you have hit a high ball and to the side after you have hit a low ball. Try to keep it looking straight ahead and you'll have good control over your volleys.

Because you must hit the ball up and still not hit it out beyond the baseline, the low volley is a difficult shot and must be played carefully.

Jab these balls as you do high volleys, but jab them much more easily. With a firm grip and a firm wrist, jab forward *and* downward with the racket face slightly open so that the strings move across the ball to give it some backspin. This downward jabbing motion will soften the impact of the ball and keep it from rebounding too hard off the racket face; the slightly opened racket face will make the ball go up and clear the net.

Play these low volleys carefully, almost babying them over the net; you can't do much with them, but at least get them back.

76

Play Low Volleys Carefully

Forehand

77

Aim Carefully When You Volley

When you are at the net and are able to make a play on your opponent's shot, you'll want to volley aggressively, of course. And so you'll aim to any opening, any hole you see in his court.

But your opponent will often be in good position, at his baseline and midway between the sidelines, leaving no opening. In this case, you must move him around to create an opening.

You can move him by hitting deep or by hitting a relatively short, sharp angle shot. Hit deep enough—and with enough force—to make your ball carry beyond his baseline after it bounces. If you angle the shot, angle it enough so that it carries across his sideline after it bounces.

This is not to say that you should always aim very close to the baseline or a sideline; you'll miss too often if you do. Give yourself some margin for error; aim far enough inside the lines to allow for some slight inaccuracy on your part. But still aim close enough to the lines to make the ball cross the lines after it bounces.

Be aggressive when volleying. Try to go forward to *intercept* the ball before it reaches you or a position to the side of you. Don't wait for the ball to come to you; go forward and meet it out in front so that you can see it hit the strings without having to turn your head to the side.

Pretend there is a line on the court about two feet in front of your volleying position, parallel to the net. As the driven ball approaches you, plan to meet it directly above this line. Step, lean, or lunge forward to meet the ball above the line and you'll add extra punch and speed to your volley.

Practice this, and as a bonus you'll discover that you begin to react more quickly and aggressively when playing at the net.

78

Go Forward to Meet the Ball

79

When at the Net, Move Toward the Ball

When you are at the net and your opponent is hitting a ground stroke from the corner of the court, be especially careful to guard against a hard-hit down-the-line shot. He's hitting into a long area if he hits down the line; he can really powder the ball to get it past you in a hurry. Move to a position to the side of the center line—toward the side the ball is on—to cut down the opening he has down the sideline and to shorten the distance you have to move to cut off this passing shot.

He can hit cross-court from the corner, too, but if he does he'll have to hit this shot easier than he does the down-the-line shot to keep the ball from going wide of the sideline, so you'll have time to get to it.

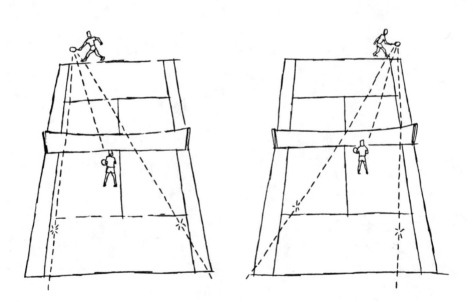

When you are at the net and your opponent cuts or slices the ball to impart backspin to it, you must allow for this spin as you volley his shot. The backspin will cause the ball to deflect downward off your racket more than a nonspinning ball would. And if the ball is already descending when you hit it, it will deflect downward even more because of its trajectory (the angle of incidence equals the angle of deflection). The downward trajectory and the spin will combine to cause the ball to be deflected downward sharply. You must allow for this deflection to avoid hitting into the net. Simply raise your sights a bit and aim for a safe margin of net clearance.

If your opponent hits with a great deal of topspin, the ball will deflect upward a bit off your racket as you volley. Make allowances for this upward deflection by lowering your sights as you volley.

80

Allow for Spin When You Volley

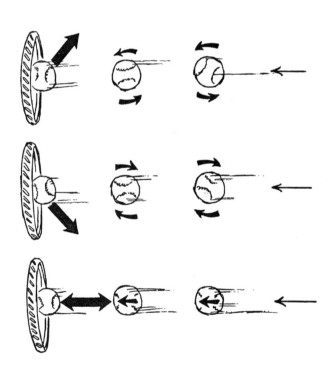

81

Use the Crossover Step When Volleying

If you're not getting to wide passing shots as quickly as you think you should, your problem might be the result of poor footwork. When you turn to hit a forehand, for example, do you pivot on your right foot while simultaneously stepping with your left foot as you should? Or do you first step away from the ball with your right foot before stepping with the left? Only the first method permits the quickness and range necessary in fast play.

If you find it difficult to correct such faulty footwork, try this. Place a racket on the ground between your feet. Straddle the racket and have a partner deliberately feed wide volleys to you. In your attempts to avoid stepping on the racket (by drawing your right foot back), you'll learn to use the right foot as a pivot as you swing your left foot to the side in a crossover step.

To reach very wide balls, practice taking a short sideward step with the right foot first and then making the crossover step with the left foot. A quick move like this will enable you to cover almost half the court (from your normal volleying position almost to the sideline).

The simple concept of making a karate jab at the ball will improve your backhand volley. Hold the racket firmly, out in front of your body and, as the ball approaches you, step toward it with your right foot and give it a firm, crisp, karate jab with the racket head. Your racket shaft should be about parallel to the ground for waist-high balls, a little more vertical for chest- and shoulder-high balls, and slanting down very slightly for low balls. Jab the high balls fairly hard (you're hitting these down), ease up a little for waist-high balls, and jab the low balls very easily and carefully (you're hitting these up). Undercut the low balls a little, jabbing the racket head forward and down across the back of the ball.

Whatever kind of ball you hit, don't flip the racket head at the ball; merely jab it forward with a firm grip and a firm wrist, trying to stop the movement of the racket immediately after the hit.

82

Karate-Jab
Your Backhand Volleys

83

Keep Your Elbow Down on Your Backhand Volley

If your backhand volleys generally go higher than you intend them to, it's probably because you're raising your elbow during the forward swing. As a result of raising your elbow, your racket head droops and the hitting surface of the racket slants skyward. You then hit the underside of the ball, causing a pop-up.

Keep your elbow down as you swing so you can make contact flush on the backside of the ball (the side farthest from the net). A good way to practice keeping your elbow down is to press a can against your body with the upper part of your hitting arm while volleying slowly tossed balls. After only a few hits in this manner you'll learn the feel of the proper elbow position and you'll be able to transfer this feel to your regular backhand volley. You will now be able to volley in an aggressive manner, slashing at the ball rather than popping it up.

Use a backhand volley to protect yourself at the net when a hard ball is hit directly at you.

If you stand in the orthodox waiting position, your racket will be almost in position to make a backhand volley. As the ball comes to you, merely move your hitting arm and elbow to the right and put the racket face directly in front of the ball; keep your grip and wrist firm and simply block the ball, letting it bounce off the racket face.

Practice these shots by having someone deliberately hit directly at you. With a little practice you'll become adept at moving your elbow and arm quickly and you'll be able to protect yourself from even the hardest hit ball.

84

Protect Yourself with a Backhand

85

Slide Away from Close Balls

When you are at the net, try to slide away from balls that come directly at you to avoid having to play them with a cramped swing.

Pretend there is a huge clock face directly in front of you as you volley. If a ball comes directly at you (along numeral 12 or numeral 6 on the clock face), quickly slide to the left so that you'll have room to swing the racket to play a normal forehand volley. By sliding away from the ball you can convert the difficult 12 and 6 o'clock shots to easier 1, 2, 3, 4, or 5 o'clock shots.

If the ball comes to you slightly on your backhand side but still at 12 or 6 o'clock, slide to the right and convert these to normal 7, 8, 9, 10, or 11 o'clock backhand volleys.

You won't always have time to slide away from these close balls, but if you do have time, keep the clock-face concept in mind and convert the difficult shots into easier ones by sliding to the side.

In fast play you don't always have time to change from forehand to backhand grips when volleying. Play is so fast that you have to volley with a no-change grip, using the same grip for both forehand and backhand shots.

The no-change grip is midway between your standard forehand and backhand grips. You'll have trouble using it at first because you're accustomed to using your left hand to support the racket as you change grips when the ball approaches you. You can break the habit of changing by practicing one-handed volleying.

Hold the racket in a no-change grip and place your nonhitting hand on your left hip. Keep your hand on your hip as you practice volleying with the other hand only. With practice you'll become adept at changing the position of your wrist and elbow as you volley. After you've broken the grip-changing habit, you can revert to using your left hand to support the racket between volleys.

86

Volley One-Handed to Learn the No-Change Grip

87

Think "Backhand" When at the Net

Unless you are an experienced player, you probably have trouble with backhand volleys, especially if you change grips from the forehand to the backhand. If you do have trouble with these shots, try waiting at the net with your backhand grip. Assume the ball will come to your backhand and be prepared both physically (with a backhand grip) and mentally (by thinking "backhand") for it. If the ball does come to your backhand, you'll be all set to play it; if it comes to your forehand instead, you can probably change very easily to the forehand grip because the grip is usually more natural and comfortable for inexperienced players.

Think "backhand" when at the net and you'll probably have much less trouble making backhand volleys.

Backhand . . .

Have you ever noticed how experienced players seem to cover the net like a blanket and allow very few balls to get past them? They've learned the secret of net play—make a quick start and don't quit.

Never assume that you cannot reach the ball. Try for everything by making a quick start and then continuing to move to the ball, even if it appears the ball will be out of your reach. Once you get started—once you've made the first step—keep going; you'll be accelerating then, gathering momentum, and you'll be moving a lot faster than you think you are and you'll get to the ball.

Once you get the habit of not quitting on these passing shots, you'll get a lot more of them back.

88

Try for Everything When at the Net

89

Practice the Drive-Volley

The drive-volley is a stroke that you should use to return slow, lazy floaters when you are at the net or in midcourt. It is an important stroke because you should be able to put these floaters away for winners, yet you probably never practice it.

Practice the stroke with a partner. Stand in midcourt, just inside the service line, and ask him to deliberately feed you slow floaters. Drive-volley these balls back to him until you get some feel for the stroke. Then stand on the baseline and run forward to play these floaters, learning to actually pounce on them when you see them coming.

Play these floaters about chest or head high, using a short-swing drive-swing (similar to your regular drive-swings but with a shorter backswing and a shorter follow-through). Keep your wrist firm and be sure to get sideways as you hit them; the tendency is to flip your wrist and to hit while facing the net too much.

To volley successfully you must be quick not only in moving to the ball but in moving your racket as well. One of the best ways of improving your reaction speed is by practicing quick-exchange volleys frequently. You and a buddy can do this by working on a drill called Speedy-V.

Stand on opposite sides of the net in volleying positions (about nine feet from the net). One of you start a rally of volleys by feeding the ball to the other player, then both of you volley the ball to each other, trying to keep it in play. Hit easily at first, merely setting the ball up for each other, then gradually pick up speed.

Regular practice in speed-volleying will increase your reaction time and eventually you will be able to move your racket very quickly.

Practice
Speed-Volleying

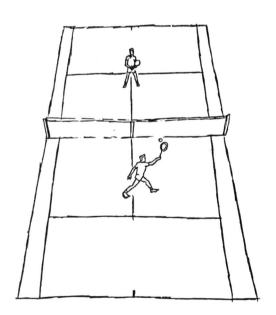

91

Develop Strength for Volleying

Though your racket weighs only a few ounces, a certain amount of strength in your hand, your wrist, and your forearm is necessary to move it quickly for fast net play.

One good way to develop the strength you need for volleying—perhaps the best way—is to volley against a wall or backboard with a cover on your racket head. The standard racket cover isn't intended for this, but it can serve as a useful prop for this kind of practice.

Use your regular volley grips, and use the same strokes you use in actual play (block, jab, punch). Recover to the ready position after each hit if you have time, or make the full change from one stroke to the other (forehand to backhand, etc.) if you don't have time to return to the ready position.

This practice procedure of volleying with a cover on the racket is in keeping with the theory of specificity in athletic training, which implies that the best way to develop strength is to practice the moves and actions that you must make in competition. In other words, the best way to develop strength for volleying is by volleying. And an even better way is volleying while having to overcome the added weight and resistance of the racket cover.

OVERHEAD SMASH

You must be able to hit consistent, forcing overhead smashes in order to get full value from your net game. Unless you can deal forcefully with lobs, your net game will be of little value to you because your opponent will lob to exploit your weak overhead when you come to the net.

Beginners often get discouraged when they first start to learn to hit overheads. The stroke is actually a simple one, being very similar to the serve. It is fairly difficult to learn, however, because it involves judgment of where the lobbed ball will come down and timing the swing so that the racket face meets the rapidly descending ball at the proper point over your head. In this section several tips are suggested that might help you learn or improve your stroke.

Overhead smash

If you have trouble hitting overhead smashes (most beginners do), it's probably because you haven't learned to time and judge the ball well.

Improve your timing and judgment by shortening your grip and playing the ball as though it were a high volley rather than an overhead smash. Use the short, high-volley swing (it's like a dart-throwing swing or a hammering-a-nail swing) and you'll make firm contact with the ball. You'll not be able to really *smash* the ball, but at least you won't swing and miss completely.

After your timing and judgment have improved, use a full grip and gradually lengthen your swing, and it won't be long before you'll be able to smash the ball with a full swing.

92

Use a Short Swing to Improve Your Overhead

93

Hit Overheads with a Compact Swing

The overhead smash swing is similar but not identical to the serve swing. The significant difference between the two is that the overhead swing is much more compact. Instead of swinging the racket down past your knees as you do when serving, simply swing the racket up and back from your ready position to hit an overhead. Sort of cock the racket up behind your right shoulder as you wait for the ball to descend. Extend your left arm toward the ball for balance (this will put your body in a "Y" position), then when the ball has fallen into hitting range complete the smash by duplicating your serve swing.

The short, compact backswing and the pause in the "Y" position as you draw a bead on the ball will enable you to time the ball well and ensure a firm hit.

You must be in position almost directly below the descending ball in order to smash lobs effectively. Learn to get below the ball by playing catch with a partner.

Stand on opposite sides of the net, each of you about 10 feet from the net, and toss high lobs back and forth to each other. Stand in the ready position as your partner tosses, then quickly turn to the sideways hitting position when the ball is in the air. Try to get directly below the falling ball to catch it, using short, quick, skipping steps. Try to get to the ball early so that you have to wait for it to fall down on you. "Hurry up and wait" is a good way to think about moving to get below the ball so that the ball would hit you on the head if you didn't catch it.

Play Catch to Learn to Judge Lobs

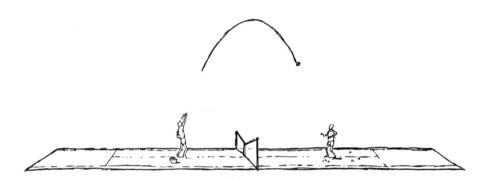

95

Use Short, Quick Steps When Smashing

When smashing a lob that requires little movement from your ready position at the net, use short, quick steps to get directly below the descending ball. Try to get below the ball so that if you didn't hit it it would hit you on the head.

Skip sideways, forward, backward, or diagonally to get below the ball; when you get to where you *think* the ball will be coming down on your head, be sure your left foot is forward and your weight is back on your rear foot. Think of this position as a temporary one and be prepared to make some last-second adjustments in it. You might misjudge the ball or the wind might alter its flight. Make whatever adjustments are necessary by skipping, then smash with power and confidence.

OVERHEAD
SMASH

If you are missing overheads, perhaps some flaw has crept into your swing. One of the most common flaws is that of bending forward at the waist during the forward swing. Bending, or jackknifing, causes you to swing down more than you intend to.

If you are bending as you smash, correct this by reaching *up* to hit the ball. Don't wait for the ball to fall down on you; go up and meet it at full stretch. Feel that you are pulling your shirttail out of your shorts as you reach and swing up and out (toward the net) at the ball.

Keeping your body straight will help keep your head steady, too, and you will be able to see the ball better and hit it more cleanly.

96

Keep Your Body Straight When Smashing

97

Flip the Racket Up and Over When Smashing

The overhead smash is usually—but not always—a power stroke; you're literally trying to smash the ball.

To get power in the stroke, use a lot of wrist and hand action. Combine this with a forward shift of weight and a good deal of arm and shoulder action and you'll be using all the sources of power you need.

During the hitting part of the swing, flip the racket head *up* and *over* at the ball rather than pulling it down across the ball. Pretend there is a face on the ball looking down at you; hit the ball on its forehead, flipping the racket head so that the back of your hand faces the sky immediately after impact and so that your racket begins to point at the ground.

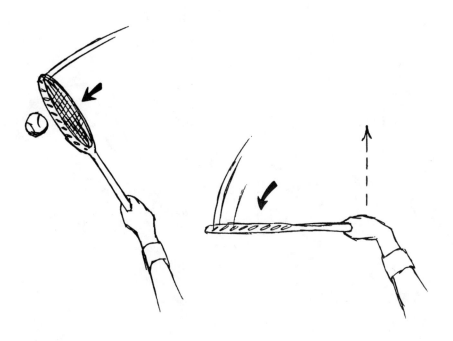

OVERHEAD
SMASH

On windy days lobs are difficult to judge, and many overhead smashes are missed that would be hit successfully on calm days.

If your opponent is lobbing against the wind, keep in mind that his lob will tend to fall shorter than you would normally expect it to. The tendency when smashing then is to hit the ball too far in front and to hit the ball down too much. Be sure to get directly below these balls.

If your opponent is lobbing with the wind, the ball will be carried deep; if you're not careful, the wind will carry the ball too far behind you for you to smash it with power.

Be conscious of the wind and its effect on lobs and compensate for it by moving under the ball, moving forward or backward as necessary, so you can smash with power.

98

Be Conscious of the Wind When Hitting Overheads

99

Let the
High Lobs Bounce

Any lob that is dropping vertically or almost vertically is difficult to smash on the fly because of the angle and speed at which it drops. Let these high lobs bounce, then smash them after they have bounced up to smashing level. Because the ball will bounce nearly vertically, you won't have to back up much to smash it; the advantage you gain by making it easier to time and judge the ball will offset the disadvantage of having to retreat a few steps to smash the ball.

If, after letting a lob bounce, you have to retreat five or six steps to smash the ball, the ball was not falling vertically and you probably should not have let it bounce. It's too late to do much about *that* after the shot, but try to remember the height and trajectory of the lob. When you get an identical lob later, remember to smash it *before* it bounces.

OVERHEAD
SMASH

MISCELLANEOUS STROKES

Although the ground strokes, the serve, and the volleys are the strokes you use most often when playing, there are additional strokes that you are sometimes forced to play which you must play well in order to have a well-rounded game. Chief among these are the lob, the half volley, the drop shot, and the drop volley.

You must learn, too, to make most effective use of your ground strokes when making approach shots, when returning the serve, and when passing a man at the net.

The lob

Vary the swing you use to lob, tailoring it to the situation. If you're lobbing from deep in the court and you want to make a high, defensive lob, use a full, long swing, carrying the ball on the strings for an instant as you *push* the ball upward and forward.

If you're lobbing from midcourt and you want to make a quick, surprise lob that barely clears your opponent at the net, use a short swing. Your ball must travel a relatively short distance so you don't need a long, full swing.

Simply block or jab hard-hit balls to lob them. A hard-hit serve, drive, or smash has sufficient speed to rebound off your racket; all you have to do is open the racket face slightly to impart a little underspin to the ball.

100

Vary Your Swing When Lobbing

101

Vary the High Point of Your Lobs

The arc of your lobs should be determined by where you lob from. If you are deep in the court and are forced to make a high, defensive lob, try to make the lob peak directly over the net. Think "defense" when you are deep and in trouble and throw up a high, lazy floater that peaks over the net. A football team punts when deep in trouble; you should also punt by lobbing, but make the ball peak directly over the net.

If your opponent is at the net and you are trying to win the point with a quick surprise, deceptive lob from inside the baseline, make the ball peak directly over his head. Hit it just high enough to clear him so he can't smash it. It's a risky shot, but it can be very effective against an opponent who crowds the net.

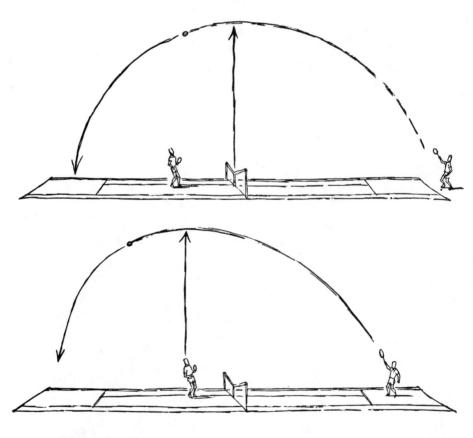

MISCELLANEOUS
STROKES

You must swing forward *and* upward to make a normal lob. The degree to which you must swing upward will depend upon a number of things, but to get a general idea of how much up motion you should put into your swing use a clock-face analogy.

As you swing to hit a forehand lob, pretend there is a clock face on the ball and simply swing to hit the ball on the numeral 4 as you swing upward toward the numeral 10. Pretend, too, that there is a huge clock face around the ball and swing from 4 to 10 on it. To make a backhand lob, reverse the clocks and swing and hit from 8 to 2.

You'll have to adjust the power of the forward motion of your racket and open the racket face slightly as you lob, but the clock-face analogy will help you to get the proper trajectory on your normal lobs.

102

Use a Clock-Face Analogy When Lobbing

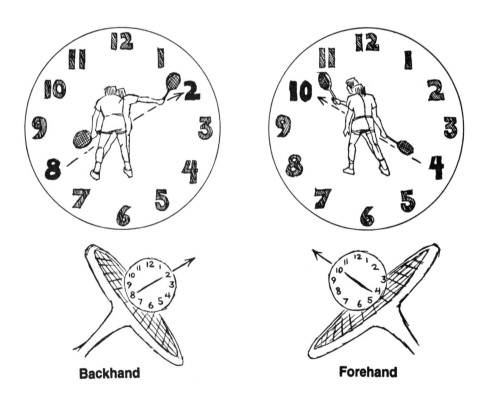

Backhand

Forehand

103

Aim Your Lobs

When you're in trouble and on the defense against a man at the net, your best play usually is to lob. At times lobbing to the center of your opponent's court might be all you can manage. At other times you might have a choice of direction.

Your best lob at times might be to his backhand side, to force him to hit a high backhand volley or a backhand smash. For this you must hit low enough to prevent him from moving around the ball to smash it with a forehand.

At other times you might be able to disregard his strokes and location and instead lob along the long cross-court dimension of the court. You'll then not have to play your shot so delicately, and the result might be a more difficult shot for your opponent to handle.

When you are in extreme trouble, lob high and deep. Think about a football team punting when faced with a troublesome situation; equate your lob to a football punt (it has a similar trajectory) and use it to get out of trouble.

 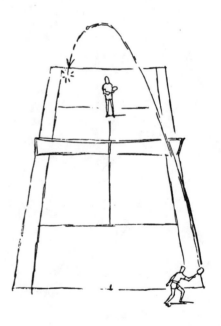

MISCELLANEOUS
STROKES

You probably seldom practice the half volley, yet it is a very important stroke, especially in doubles. You are usually forced to make the shot following a serve and an approach to the net or when you get caught in midcourt.

Practice the shot by standing on the service line and returning balls driven at your feet by a buddy. In actual play, you would move forward to the normal volleying position after making the half volley from midcourt, but for practice stay on the service line so that you get repeated practice in making the shot.

Practice both forehand and backhand half volleys. They are difficult shots, but as you practice your judgment and timing will improve, and you'll soon learn to be comfortable while making the shots.

104

Practice the Half Volley

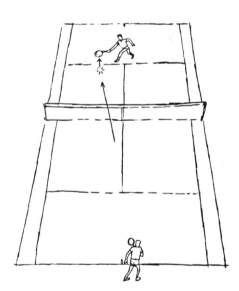

105

Use an Abbreviated Ground Stroke to Half-Volley

Think of the half volley as an abbreviated ground stroke; use a short backswing and a long, but not full, follow-through. Move the racket straight back behind the point at which you judge the ball will land, then, keeping your wrist firm, move the racket straight forward and slightly upward, hitting the ball just after it bounces. Bend your knees to get down low so that you can make a sideways swing rather than a vertical one.

You'll have to fool around with the angle of the racket face as you swing, tilting it up or down according to the needs of the situation. Experience will teach you how much to tilt it and whether to tilt it up or down.

You can play half volleys accurately if you hit the ball immediately after it bounces. These shots become increasingly difficult to play if you let them rise more than a few inches after they bounce.

One way to learn to hit quickly after the bounce is to be attentive to the sounds associated with the shot—the sound of the ball bouncing on the court and the sound of the racket meeting the ball. To play the shot effectively, make the sounds occur quickly one after the other.

A good analogy to use as you practice the shot is the expression a baby uses to refer to his daddy: "da-da." Make your half volleys sound like that, with the sound of the hit occurring immediately after the sound of the bounce.

106

Listen to Your Half Volleys

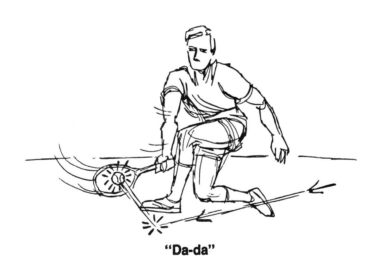

"Da-da"

107

To Drop-Volley, Bunt

A drop volley is a volley that lands very close to the net, falling almost vertically, and then bounces almost vertically. To make such a shot, you must cushion the impact of the ball on the racket so that the ball almost plops off the strings. Don't jab or punch the racket face at the ball; instead, draw it backward a bit precisely at impact to deaden the impact.

The stroke is very similar to that used by a baseball batter when he bunts the ball. He cushions the bat by holding it loosely and drawing it backward a bit just as the ball strikes it. Do the same thing with your racket as the ball strikes it.

When learning the shot, first practice bunting the ball to yourself so that you can catch it with your nonhitting hand. Then bunt a little harder to make the ball barely clear the net. Finally, cup your racket face as you bunt (turn the top edge of the racket face back a bit) to give the ball some backspin so that it won't bounce*forward after it lands.

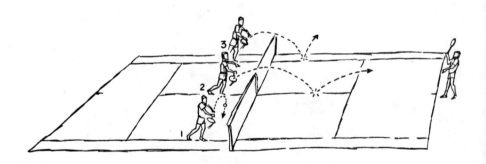

MISCELLANEOUS
STROKES

To drop-volley effectively, loosen your grip and soften your wrist to deaden the force of impact of the ball on the racket. The ball will then leave your racket with little force and speed and drop short in your opponent's court.

To learn how easily this can be done, try this experiment: As a friend hits to you from his baseline, volley back to him while holding your racket between your first two fingers and your thumb. As you meet the ball, your racket will recoil rather than move forward. The result will be a soft shot, one that dribbles back to your friend, the kind of shot that would win for you in actual play.

In play you'll have to hold the racket firmly to move it quickly to intercept the ball. But even then loosen your grip as the racket meets the ball and you'll hit softly enough to merely drop the ball over the net.

108

Loosen Your Grip to Drop-Volley

109

**Plan Your Drop Shots
Carefully**

The best time to use the drop shot is when you are hitting from inside your baseline while your opponent is behind his baseline.

If you drop-shot from *behind* your baseline, the ball must travel a long way to clear the net; most likely he'll have running time to reach the ball. And if you try the shot when he's *inside* his baseline, he'll not have very far to run to reach it.

Be aware of *your* location and *his* location before you make a drop shot. For the shot to be effective, you must be short in the court and he must be long. If you drop-shot at any other time, most often you will lose the point, regardless of how good your drop shot is.

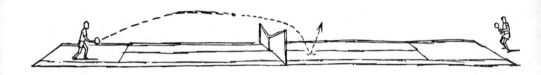

*MISCELLANEOUS
STROKES*

When you make a short, well-placed drop shot, one that you think your opponent will be barely able to reach, it may be to your advantage to move forward in your court a step or two to intercept his return with a volley. He'll have to scramble for the ball and he'll probably not be able to do much with his return. If you are alert to this, you can pounce on the return and volley the ball past him.

As you plan this tactic you must assess the effectiveness of your drop shot. If you hit it too strong and the ball carries toward your opponent after it bounces, he will have a fairly easy shot to make. In this case you're better off defending against it from your backcourt. But if you hit the drop shot softly and perhaps even with backspin to make the ball bounce vertically, he'll have a difficult shot. Moving forward to intercept his return may then be the best play.

110

Be Prepared to Volley After Making a Good Drop Shot

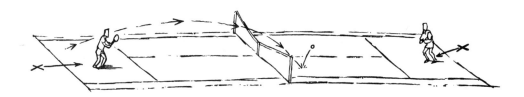

111

Experiment to Find Your Best Receiving Location

When receiving the serve, vary your position to accommodate the speed of the serve. Against a fast serve stand a step or so behind the baseline. Against easier serves stand in closer, either on the baseline or inside it.

Standing behind the baseline allows you more time to react to the serve, but it also forces you to cover a wider angle. Standing inside the baseline reduces the angle you have to cover, but it also allows you less time to react to the serve.

Experiment during play to find your best location. Stand close, stand deep, stand a little right, stand a little left. One of these locations will be the best one for you to use to make your opponent's serve less effective.

MISCELLANEOUS
STROKES

If you're having trouble returning hard serves because you can't change grips quickly from forehand to backhand, perhaps you're using the wrong grip as a waiting grip.

Practice returning hard serves using a forehand grip as a waiting grip. Can you change quickly to the backhand grip when you have to? Perhaps you can. But try waiting with a backhand grip; maybe you can change more quickly to the forehand grip.

And finally, try waiting with an in-between grip halfway between your forehand and backhand grips. You'll now have to move your hand only halfway to hit either a forehand or a backhand; this might be the quickest way for you to change.

There's no set rule about which grip you should use as a waiting grip. Experiment a bit; try each of the three grips suggested above and discover which works best for *you.*

112

Discover Your Best Waiting Grip

113

Hit High-Bouncing Serves on the Rise

If your opponent continually serves high-bouncing spin serves and follows them to the net, move forward to hit these balls as they rise after the bounce. You'll be hitting the ball earlier than you would be if you were to play back behind the baseline to play the ball as it descends. Because you hit earlier, your shot will get back to him sooner, giving him less time to reach a good volleying location. You'll then have a better chance of making him hit at a low ball, one that he cannot volley as aggressively as a high ball from a location closer to the net. As a result, most often you'll have an easier ball to play on your next attempt to pass him.

Playing the ball on the rise demands good timing and quick reflexes, but with practice you can learn to do it. Make a point of practicing this regularly.

MISCELLANEOUS
STROKES

When your opponent serves and stays in the backcourt, try to force him well behind his baseline with your return of serve. If you force him back, he'll have to make a long shot, one that must travel a long distance to land deep in your court. You should have very little difficulty getting to this long shot.

Place a majority of these deep returns to your opponent's backhand. Eight out of ten average players have weaker backhands than forehands, and the remaining two players cannot attack when hitting backhands from behind their baselines. Your tactics then should be as simple as this: Make your opponent go backward to hit a backhand. When you succeed at this, you will already have begun to control the rally, which means, of course, that you are already on your way toward winning the point.

114

Return Serves
Deep to the Backhand

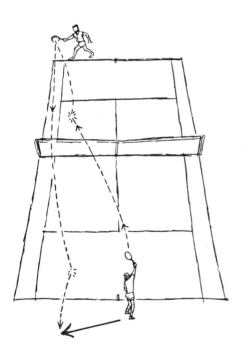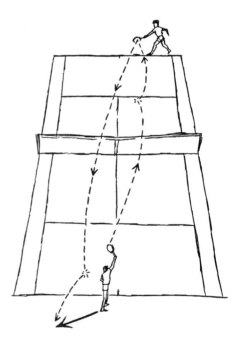

115

Use a Short-Radius Swing to Return Serves

You'll be able to move your racket quickly when returning serves if you use what is known as a short-radius swing.

Stand in the normal ready position, supporting your racket with your left hand holding the racket throat and the right hand grasping the handle in whatever grip you use for returning serves. Instead of reaching forward so that your elbows are in front of you, however, place your elbows close to the side of your hips.

With your elbows at your sides rather than in front of you, you'll shorten the radius of your backswing. You'll then need less force to overcome the inertia of the racket and you'll have more force available to move the racket fast. As a result, you'll be able to make a faster backswing, one that might give you a play on serves that otherwise might be too fast for you.

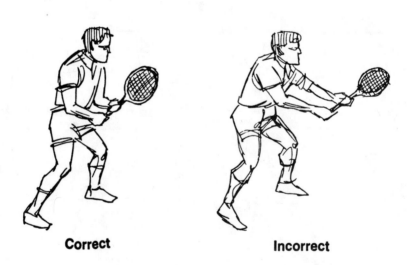

Correct   **Incorrect**

To defend effectively against a good net-rushing server, vary your returns. Mix drives with slices, mix cross-court and center shots with down-the-line placements.

When you aim down the line you can hit short or deep and still place your shot out of your opponent's reach. But when you aim cross-court, you must hit to the short corner (where the service line meets the sideline) to place the ball out of his reach.

Lob often enough to keep him guessing about your intentions. Make him suspect that you *might* lob. He'll then not run forward very aggressively and as a result your drives and slices are likely to be more effective.

116

Vary Your Shots When Receiving

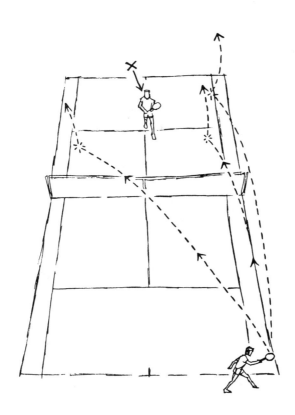

117

Cut Off the Angle When Returning Serves

When returning widely angled serves, cut down the angle by moving to the side *and* forward, moving perpendicular to the line of flight of the ball. As you move forward not only will you cut down the angle, but you'll make a more aggressive return as well because your body weight will be moving forward into the shot.

As you move perpendicular to the line of flight you'll probably have to play many balls on the rise. Hitting on the rise is not the easiest way to play the ball, but with practice you can learn to do it.

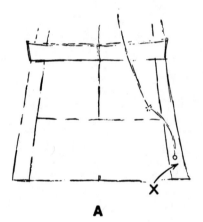

A

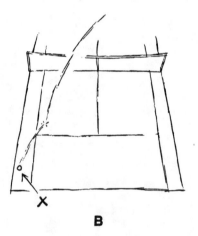

B

MISCELLANEOUS STROKES

Improve your ability to return hard, "killer" serves by making a special effort to practice returning them. Ask a partner who has a big serve to serve to you so you can practice returns. Don't play points, merely drill on returns—he serves, you return.

If you can't find a partner who has a big serve, find the hardest server you can and ask him to serve to you, but have him serve from six feet inside the baseline. His served ball will reach you in less time than if he served from behind the baseline, and it will come at you from a higher point (at a greater angle) pretty much like a hard serve would come at you if served from behind the baseline. His serve will be converted into a hard-hit one. As you drill on returning his serves you'll improve your ability to return big serves in play.

118

Drill on Returning Killer Serves

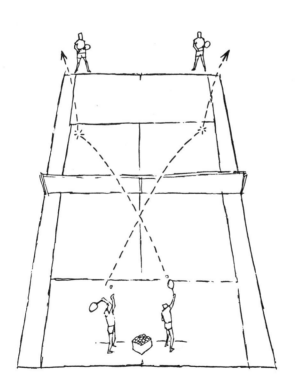

119

Plan Your Approach to the Net

Your net attack is more likely to be successful when you make an aggressive approach shot to your opponent's weak stroke. But the location from which you make the shot is important, too. If you hit and run to the net from a position behind your baseline, you'll probably have to volley from no man's land (from near the service line); from this deep position your volleys will have less sting than you'd like. A more effective way is to go to the net only from inside your baseline. You'll then be able to volley from inside the service line or even closer to the net. From there you can hit aggressively on your first shot and then move forward to an even better position for the next shot.

If you play on two-tone red and green courts, you can use the contrasting colors as cues for going to the net. When hitting from the red area (behind the baseline) stay back. Red means "stop"! When hitting from the green area (inside the baseline), go to the net if you can make an aggressive shot. Green means "go"!

MISCELLANEOUS
STROKES

When your tactical plan is to go to the net to finish off a rally with a volley, be patient. Wait until you can hit from a location inside your baseline and when you can use your stronger stroke.

If, instead, you run to the net from behind your baseline, you may be forced to handle a difficult low ball from behind your service line. And, if you go to the net behind a weak shot, your opponent is likely to have an easy ball to play on his attempt to pass you. In neither case will you be able to continue to press your attack.

A more effective way is to wait for a safe chance to attack. Perhaps you can attack only on your forehand, for example, and only when hitting from a step or two inside your baseline.

Aggressiveness is usually the winning way, but only when tempered with good judgment.

120

Be Patient
When Attacking

121

Learn the Running Forehand Approach Shot

When your opponent gives you a short forehand, pounce on the ball, moving up quickly so you can play the ball at belt level. Then drive the ball deep to his backhand and advance to the net behind the shot, hitting the ball flat or with moderate topspin.

Learn to make this shot on-the-run, hitting the ball while you are running forward. This is tricky, but with practice you can learn to do it.

Hit the ball while taking a forward running step. Your left foot should be in midair, moving forward toward the net, at the moment of ball contact. Your right foot should be swung forward immediately after the left foot is planted firmly as you continue running to the net.

This running forehand approach shot will enable you to get to the net more quickly than if you were to stop and hit the ball. It will get you into the habit of looking for the short ball and taking advantage of it, too, and make you into a more opportunistic player.

MISCELLANEOUS
STROKES

Take advantage of a short ball to your backhand—hit the ball deep and advance to the net behind the shot.

Don't try to drive these balls as you do short forehands, however. You should be moving forward as you play the ball, and you'll have difficulty making a fairly long swing. You must get sideways to the net to play these shots, and the necessary footwork prevents you from taking the racket back far enough to drive the ball.

Play these shots the way most of the top players do—slice or chip the ball instead of driving it. You'll not be able to hit the ball hard, so don't try to. All you should be trying to do is get to the net, and the slice or chip will give you good control over the ball. And because the ball will not travel fast, you will have ample time to reach a good volleying position.

122

Slice or Chip Your Backhand Approach Shots

123

Hit Approach Shots Parallel to the Sidelines

A good rule of thumb when you make an approach shot off a short ball is this: Hit the ball parallel to the sidelines.

If you get a short ball on your forehand side, hit the ball deep to your opponent's *backhand* corner, hitting parallel to the sideline. If you get a short ball on your backhand side, hit the ball deep to your opponent's *forehand* corner, again hitting parallel to the sideline.

By hitting parallel to the sidelines, you cut down the distance you have to travel to be in good volleying position at the net; you have to advance only to the near side of the center line. If you hit your shot cross-court instead, you have to advance to the far side of the center line, clearly a greater distance which you would probably not be able to traverse quickly enough to cut off the hard-hit down-the-line passing shot.

If one of your opponent's strokes is considerably weaker than the other, you should make an exception to this rule and hit your approach shot to this weak side. The greater distance you'll have to travel to be in good volleying position will be more than offset by forcing him to play his weak shot.

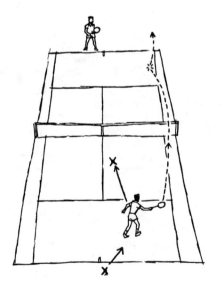 

MISCELLANEOUS
STROKES

When you are approaching the net behind a ground stroke or a well-placed serve, most likely your opponent will not hit the ball directly to you. He has several choices of good shots—he can hit to your forehand or backhand sides, he can lob over your head, or he can hit the ball low at your feet. As he hits, you must be ready to move to the ball so that you can play it.

Watch your opponent as you run up, and just as he begins to make his backswing, hop to a *ready* position. The location in the court where you should make this hop will vary, depending upon how hard you hit the ball, how fast you run, and how deep you were when you hit the ball. You should try to get as close to the ideal volleying position as you can, but more important than getting close is being ready to move to the ball. So make a ready-hop just as he begins his swing.

Think of this little hop (it's similar to the one children make when playing hopscotch) as a *ready* hop. Hop to a feet-spread, knees-slightly-bent position (the ready position), holding the racket in front of you. As the ball leaves your opponent's racket, push off in whichever direction you have to in order to get to the ball.

If you are a beginner, actually come to a stop in the ready position after making the hop. Then move to the ball when you see where it is going. As you gain experience and improve your footwork, you'll learn to rebound from the hop so quickly that you'll make a barely perceptible pause in the ready position and immediately push off toward the ball.

124

Make a Ready-Hop When Coming Up

125

Vary Your Steps When Coming Up

If your opponent consistently makes low, short service returns that you have difficulty volleying when you come up behind your serve, get tricky—vary the number of steps you take before making your ready-hop. Sometimes run in fast and far, as far as you can get before he starts his backswing. Other times make your ready-hop after only two or three steps to let his short return bounce up to you so you can play an easy-to-handle ground stroke. If he becomes aware of your tactics and returns the ball deeper, resume running in all the way to intercept his returns with volleys.

Try to keep your opponent guessing about your intentions. Don't give him a consistent target (such as the service line) to aim at every time. Don't let him groove one return; force him to make many different returns.

Two-step approach

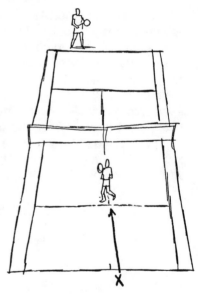

Three-step approach

MISCELLANEOUS STROKES

When hitting a sideline approach shot or a passing shot, give yourself some margin of safety; don't aim too close to the lines unless you absolutely have to. If you aim very close to the line, you could hit out even when barely missing your aiming point.

If you were to plot the landing positions of a number of your shots, you would find that some misses will be to the right of the target while others will be to the left, and that some will be long of the target while others will be short. The majority of your misses will be the result of a frequent or constant error in your stroke which causes the ball to go either right or left of the target, or short or long of it.

In either case, if your target is *very* close to the line, many of your shots will land close to the target but still be out. But if you aim at a target point a little farther from the line, many of the shots that miss the target will still be in.

Aim carefully, but select a target area that provides a safe margin for error. In this way you'll be making the percentages work to your advantage.

126

Give Yourself a Margin of Safety

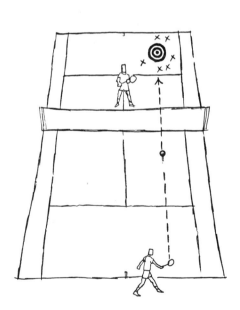

127

Make an Outside-In Approach Shot

You can combine a little backspin with a little sidespin to make effective approach shots. All you have to do to do this is use an outside-in stroke.

Hit the ball a glancing blow, meeting it on its backside (the side farthest from the net) while moving your racket across the ball from right to left and slightly downward. The right-to-left action imparts sidespin to the ball; the downward action imparts backspin to it. The sidespin will curve the ball toward your opponent's backhand corner and make it skid to his left as it bounces, and at the same time the backspin will make the ball skid low and fast.

The right-to-left motion is called an outside-in swing. Your racket moves from outside the line of flight of the approaching ball (the right side of the line as you face the ball) to inside the line (the left side of it).

This shot is best used to attack a right-handed player's backhand. A low skidding bounce is difficult for even the best of players to handle. It is a tricky shot, but with practice you can learn to make it.

The ball actually flattens out against the strings of the racket for an instant as it is hit. The longer you can keep the ball on the strings, the more control you will have over the shot. Here are some concepts that might help you keep it on the strings:

- Try to "hit the ball for a long time."
- Feel that you are steering the ball in the direction you want it to go.
- Visualize the ball as having a magnet in it; as the ball rebounds off the racket face, the magnet pulls the racket forward.
- Think of hitting not only the real ball but four or five imaginary balls, also, all in line with and connected to the real ball. Swing your racket face through all of the balls.

Use whichever concept you want to; they're all intended to get you to swing your racket straight ahead during impact and not across to the side. You'll hit the ball solidly and have good control over it when you do swing straight ahead.

128

Try to Keep the Ball on the Strings for Control

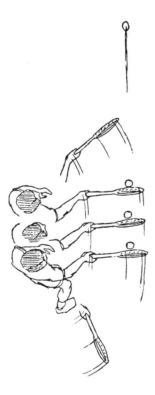

129

Play Cat and Mouse with a Volleyer

When playing in the backcourt against a man at the net, you must first "jerk him around" before you try to pass him. You must create an opening for a passing shot by playing cat and mouse with him; tease him by giving him some short cross-courts to move him out of position and keep him from crowding the net by making him aware that you might lob on occasion.

When you create an opening by moving him out of position, be alert for a weak, short shot. If he gives you one, pounce on it quickly, moving forward to play it before it drops. Hit this ball hard, but carefully, through the opening for a winner.

Don't be impatient when your opponent is at the net and try to pass him too quickly. Sometimes you'll have to hit three or four balls to create an opening before you can pass him.

MISCELLANEOUS STROKES

To play effectively above the intermediate level, you must be an all-court player—you must be skilled at backcourt play *and* at forecourt play. You must be able to play steady backcourt tennis when necessary and to play aggressive attacking tennis when necessary.

Like most players, you probably prefer one style of play to the other. If you're a backcourt player, it's probably because you enjoy that style and because you feel comfortable playing it. If you're a net rusher, it's probably because this style is fun for you and because you're comfortable playing it. In either case, you have probably never given yourself a chance to see if you can learn both styles.

Try the uncomfortable style; you might like it. During your practice sessions, deliberately force yourself to play it. If you're a backcourt player, rush to the net at every opportunity. Pretend you're the world's greatest volleyer and try to win by playing at the net.

If you are a net rusher by preference or habit, force yourself to stay in the backcourt and play steady tennis. Pretend you're the world's steadiest player.

By forcing yourself to play the nonpreferred style, you'll improve at it. And as you improve, you'll enjoy it more and want to do it more. You'll then be on your way to becoming a truly good all-court player.

130

Practice the All-Court Game

I don't volley well, so today I'm going to rush to the net at every opportunity.

131

Practice by Playing Points, Not Games

You will improve your game if you spend a lot of time during your practice sessions by playing points rather than by always playing games. Don't always "serve 'em up" when you go out on the court; take some time regularly to *practice*.

Get your practice partner to agree that you and he are going to play, but that you're not going to keep score while you play. Play point after point without keeping score. One of you serve every point for a while, then the other, and so on.

By playing points and not keeping score, you'll not be playing under pressure. With no score to worry about, there'll be no critical or crisis points to cause you to tighten up; you'll be free to try the right shots for whatever tactical situations arise. You'll learn to make these shots, and you'll acquire the confidence to make them later in actual play when you do "serve 'em up."

132

Play at
<u>Your</u> Comfortable Pace

Some players like to play at a fast pace. Between points they are always in a hurry to get back into action. Because they're accustomed to playing in a hurry, they play best at this fast pace. Psychologists would say they are playing in their comfort zone.

Other players like to play at a slow pace. They take their time between points, moving slowly, leisurely, and deliberately. Their comfort zone is a slow-moving pace.

Early in a match discover what pace your opponent seems to prefer, then try to make him play at a different pace. Force him to play out of his comfort zone. If he prefers a slow pace, speed things up by moving quickly. Perhaps he'll try to accommodate you and speed up, too. If he does, he'll be playing out of his comfort zone and will probably not play as well as he normally does.

If your opponent prefers a fast pace, slow things down. Don't deliberately stall (the rules prohibit this, but they don't require you to play at your opponent's pace), but move slowly. Take your time, make him wait. Force him to play out of his comfort zone and he'll probably not play up to his normal level.

133

Minimize Your Errors

To prevent your opponent from attacking during a baseline rally, you must hit deep into his court.

You can get depth on your shots by hitting hard. But if you hit very hard, you'll have to aim for only a minimum of net clearance to keep your shots from clearing the baseline. This combination of hard hitting and minimum net clearance might result in more errors than you can afford to make.

A better way to get depth is to hit at only moderate speed and to aim your shots so that they clear the net by three or four feet or so. This will increase your margin for error, and you won't miss as many shots as you would by hitting hard and low. The combination of ample net clearance and moderate speed will give you the depth you need with minimum risk.

**Stay Out of
No Man's Land**

The area between your baseline and your service line is often referred to as "no man's land" or "the danger zone." It is considered dangerous territory in which to be caught while your opponent is making a shot because he can hit the ball at your feet and cause you to make a difficult shot.

When you run to the net, try to reach at least your service line before having to stop or slow down to volley. In other words, run *through* no man's land; don't get caught in it. The only time you should risk volleying from no man's land is after you have hit a very aggressive serve. Your opponent is then likely to make a fairly easy return, or at least not an aggressive one. But even then move forward to a safer volleying position after you make the first volley—move inside your service line.

You can't always avoid being caught in no man's land; sometimes you're forced to play from there. Try to avoid being caught there, however, by being careful about when you go up to the net.

135

Don't Always Try to Pass a Net Man

If your opponent rushes to the net a lot, try to reduce your errors on your passing shots. Make him show that he can volley (and smash) well enough to beat you; don't beat yourself by trying to pass him all the time and missing the difficult passing shots.

Cut your errors down and force him to volley. Make him *win* the point by forcing him to make a shot—any shot! Don't *give* the point to him by trying—and missing—a difficult passing shot.

Of course, if he volleys very well, you will have to try difficult passing shots. But don't try foolish, reckless ones. You don't have to hit spectacular winners; you merely have to give him difficult balls to volley. He might miss these or pop them up; you can then pass him on the next shot.

MISCELLANEOUS
STROKES

When you're in a baseline rally, be attentive to what your opponent is doing to the ball as he hits it. If he cuts or slices it or spins it in any way, you must make allowances for this spin as you play the ball.

If he slices and his shot travels in a high trajectory, the ball will bounce slowly and more toward the vertical than if it had no spin. If he slices and the ball travels in a low trajectory (or in a line drive), the ball will skid and remain low as it bounces. And if he hits at a low ball and drags his racket across the back of the ball, the ball will bounce in the opposite direction from which his racket is moving (if his racket is moving toward your right side, the ball will bounce to your left).

Be aware of the kind of spin your opponent puts on the ball and be prepared to play the ball accordingly. Spin should bother you somewhat—it does affect the bounce of the ball—but it should never fool you.

136

Be Aware of the Spin on the Ball

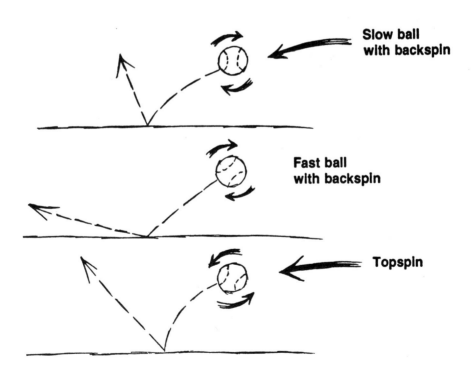

Slow ball with backspin

Fast ball with backspin

Topspin

137

Mix Lobs with Passing Shots

Try to discover early in a match how well your opponent can smash, then decide how often you will lob to him.

As you make a play on his approach shot, he'll usually be back too far for you to lob over him. But when he closes in after his first volley, he'll be more vulnerable to a lob. If you can, disguise your second shot. Look as though you're going to drive the ball, then, at the last second, lob it instead, forcing him to smash from deep in the court.

After you've done this several times and he knows you might do it again when he comes up, he'll be reluctant to close in as much as he was doing previously. Your low shots and your passing shots will now be much more effective.

Don't forget to drive his smashes back at him, too, after your lob has forced him to smash from midcourt.

MISCELLANEOUS
STROKES

When your opponent is at the net and you force him to make a half volley, anticipate a weak, short return. He isn't likely to be able to hit a crisp, deep shot, so move forward into your court a step or so even before he hits, to take advantage of his weak return. When he does give you a short ball, move in quickly to get it waist or chest high after it bounces and hit it past him.

If he gives you a slow, easy floater, move in very quickly and use your drive-volley to hit past him. Moving in this way will rush him; he'll not have sufficient time to recover after making the half volley.

And if he should make a crisp, deep shot, you will have ample time to hurry back and play the ball as a normal forehand or backhand drive.

Anticipate a weak return when your opponent half-volleys and be prepared to take advantage of it. You have him in trouble when you hit low at his feet; don't let him wriggle out of this difficult situation.

138

Hit Low and Move Forward

139

Don't Hug
Your Baseline

When playing from the baseline, try to avoid having to hit a half volley or a low, rising ball. Whenever time permits, skip or run back a step or two to let the ball bounce up to a convenient height so you can make a fuller swing at the ball.

There's a good reason for going back and giving ground this way. It's more difficult to hit low, rising balls, and you're likely to make weak, short returns. Your opponent then will be in a position to attack, and you will have lost any advantage gained by maintaining your position at the baseline. But when you move back to let the ball rise to waist height, for example, you gain time to make a normal stroke at a ball more to your liking than the low riser. As a result, you'll probably be able to play the shot more aggressively.

MISCELLANEOUS
STROKES

Your opponent's best-looking stroke or shot may not be his steadiest. For example, his flashy, spectacular forehand may be more erratic than his slower, steadier backhand. If he misses more shots there than he makes, it might be to your advantage to play to it.

Evaluate your opponent's strokes in terms of percentages. If he hits only an occasional crowd-pleasing winner with a certain stroke—and misses two out of three attempts—let him use this stroke, willingly trading him one for two.

It's not uncommon for an intermediate player to have a flashy forehand return of serve, but one that is also an inconsistent one. His backhand return might be a carefully sliced one, hit deep if you stay back or at your feet if you come up. In this case, you might be better off serving to his flashy but erratic forehand rather than to his steady, consistent backhand. Again, consider the percentages.

140

Consider
the Percentages

141

Play According to the Score

The use of the no-ad and tie-breaker methods of scoring has made tennis much less of an endurance contest than it used to be. But a smart player recognizes that certain points are still much more important than others. He therefore paces himself according to the importance of the points. He plays some points with great determination and plays others with a halfhearted effort, depending upon the score.

Following are the important points—the clutch points—which you should try your darndest to win:

—Any *game* point you have, regardless of who is serving. Go all-out for this point, trying hard to win it, to get that game in the bag.

—You're serving, 15-30 or 30-40. Winning this point will put you on even terms with your opponent. Moreover, because he has lost his lead if you win this point, he might choke on the next point.

—The first point after a long rally. Both you and your opponent are usually physically and mentally tired after a long rally, and the tendency is to let down during the next point, play it loosely, and lose it. If *you* don't let down, most often you can win this point fairly easily.

MISCELLANEOUS STROKES

If you're playing against a very tall, gangling player and he's handling your best hard-hit serves better than you'd like him to, it might be because you're serving wide to him. Because of his extremely long arms, he's usually able to reach practically all wide serves. Moreover, because of the great leverage he can generate because he is loose and lanky, he can return these balls with good speed.

Try serving your hard ball directly at this player. Try to crowd him, forcing him to play the ball close to his body. This might not nullify his hard service returns completely, but it could take some of the sting out of many of them. Because he'll not be able to take a full swing at the ball, he'll have to chip or block the ball back, thus giving you an easier ball to volley.

Try hitting the ball directly at a tall player when he's at the net and you're hitting from 6 or 7 feet inside the baseline, too. He'll have difficulty moving to the side—most tall players are really not quick movers—and he'll have to defend himself with a block volley. Be alert to pounce on this volley if it is weak and short.

142

Hit the Ball _at_ a Tall Player

143

Attack Your Opponent's Weak Stroke

If your opponent has a built-in weakness, take advantage of it. Serve to it, return serves to it, and attack it with your ground strokes. And whenever you're in trouble, hit to it.

Be careful that you don't hit to this weakness so often that his weak stroke improves during play, however. It might be best to delay your attack against this weakness until a crucial point, or a crucial shot within a point, arises.

For example, if his backhand is his weakness (most average club players have weaker backhands than forehands) and if you can rally even with him when hitting to his forehand, play a good number of your shots there. But when you get a short ball and decide to attack, attack his weak backhand.

Vary your response to the drop shot to conform to the situation; you should, however, hit it straight ahead of you most often.

If you can get to the drop shot fairly comfortably and your opponent stays back (you can see him in the periphery of your vision), your best shot is a semifloater straight in front of you; you will then be in good position to play his return. Occasionally you can drop-shot right back, hitting the ball directly in front of you to make him scramble for a low ball that you can volley for a winner.

If you barely get to his drop shot, scoop it deep in front of you if he stays back. If he moves inside his baseline hoping to drive-volley your return, try to make him hit a half volley; hit the ball straight ahead but make it bounce opposite where he is standing.

As a rule of thumb, return drop shots straight ahead of you. Only rarely, when you can drive the ball at waist level or nearly at waist level, should you hit it cross-court.

144

Return Drop Shots Straight Ahead

145

Lower Your Arm When Playing Low Balls

Forget the old bromide of "Never drop your racket head below the level of your wrist." It's impossible to play very low balls without dropping your racket head.

The trick in playing low balls is to drop the racket head and still maintain wrist and grip strength. This you can do by decreasing the angle of your arm at the shoulder by *lowering your arm* toward the ground rather than by loosening your grip or "rounding" your wrist. Lowering your arm will enable you to maintain the same forearm-wrist-racket angle you use for high balls. Your racket head will be below the level of your wrist but you'll still have strength enough to hit with power and control.

Try not to have to drop your racket head for low balls; but, if you must for very low balls, do so by lowering your arm rather than by changing your wrist angle.

Correct   **Incorrect**

On a normal ground stroke—waist high or so—you should be stepping and leaning into the ball. Your back should be fairly straight but you should be leaning toward the ball somewhat.

Reverse this lean for high balls. If you are stroking a ball at shoulder height or higher, *lean away* from the ball, bending backward a bit at the waist. You have to raise you arm at the shoulder to hit these high balls, and if you're bent over at the waist, even to the slightest degree, you won't be able to raise your arm properly; you'll probably raise your elbow and destroy your swing pattern. Don't *fall* back on these high balls; step into them with your front foot, but *lean* backward a bit at the waist so that you can raise your arm at the shoulder and take a vigorous swing at the ball.

146

Lean Away from High Balls

147

**Watch the Ball,
but Keep Your Mind
on Your Opponent**

If you're not passing a net man as often as you should when hitting passing shots from well inside the baseline, it could be because he's outguessing you. He knows he's in trouble because you're hitting from inside the baseline, so he gambles by trying to guess where you're going to hit the ball. If he guesses right and moves before you hit the ball, he manages to cut off your passing shots.

To counteract his guessing, watch the ball as you hit it, but *keep your mind on him*. You can see him out of the corner of your eye. Keep your mind on him, and if he moves before you hit, you'll be aware of which way he is moving; you'll then be able to hit the ball away from the direction he moves.

*MISCELLANEOUS
STROKES*

When you are forced back well behind your baseline to play a ground stroke, your shot must travel a long distance in order to land deep in your opponent's court. To hit deep, then, you must aim considerably higher than when hitting from near the baseline. Were you to swing in the same plane and use the same trajectory from back near the fence that you use when hitting from near the baseline, most likely your ball would hit the net or, at best, land short in your opponent's court.

When you swing from deep in the court, swing in an upward plane so that the ball travels in a higher trajectory than it does in a normal baseline drive. Aim the ball well above the net and let gravity pull it down deep in your opponent's court.

148

Aim Higher When You Are Deep

149

Mix Them Up Against a Poacher

An effective way to deal with a poacher in doubles is to turn the tables on him. Try to make him worry as much about whether you're going to hit cross-court or down the line as you do about whether or not he is going to poach.

Hit a lot of service returns at him or down the line. Don't try for winners on these shots; merely let him know you can and will hit the ball there often. If he poaches when you do hit one there, he'll look mighty foolish when the ball goes through the opening he left. After this has happened a few times, he'll be sure to curtail his poaching, and you can revert to hitting more normal cross-court returns as you quit worrying about him.

To be effective against a man at the net, you must be able to hit short cross-court shots to the short corners (the junctions of the service line and the singles sidelines). Not always will this shot pass a net man, but it will force him to make a difficult low volley and open the court for a hard passing shot.

Practice this shot regularly. Have a friend volley from the normal volleying position while you play in the backcourt and try to hit every ball to one of the short corners. You will soon learn what combination of speed and topspin you need to make the ball land short, and you'll be able to move the volleyer around, keeping him off-balance.

After you have learned to make the shot fairly well, take advantage of his weak returns. Draw him out of position by hitting to a short corner, then pounce on his return and hit it past him for a winner.

150

Learn the Short Corner Shot

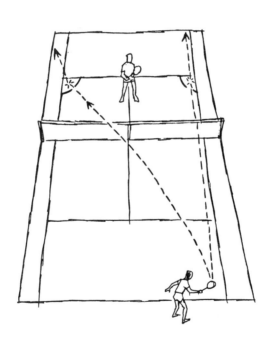

151

Hit the Top Half of a Short High Ball

Your should hit short, high-bouncing balls with topspin so that you have a safe margin for error on the shot.

Hurry to the short ball so that you can play it at chest or shoulder level, then hit down on it somewhat, feeling that you are hitting the top half of the ball as you swing forward and slightly downward. Lowering your left shoulder so that the upper part of your body tilts toward the net will help you get the feeling of hitting the top half of the ball. Your forearm and racket face will roll over a little at impact, causing the strings of the racket to brush across the top of the ball putting some topspin on it.

MISCELLANEOUS STROKES

Your intentions and choice of shots against a net man should depend, in part, on your location in the court. If you are hitting from behind the baseline, your best play may be to your opponent's feet for the purpose of getting another and safer chance to pass him. If you are hitting from inside your baseline, you may be able to pass him outright.

But there are other points to consider to determine your choice of direction. Play to the percentages and try your most consistent shot (cross-court or down the line?) more often than an erratic one. And if you hit cross-court, aim to the short corner (where the service line intersects the singles sideline). A deeper shot is likely to be within your opponent's reach. Shots down the line may be out of his reach whether you hit them short or deep.

152

Choose Your Passing Shots Carefully

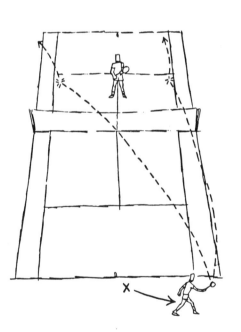

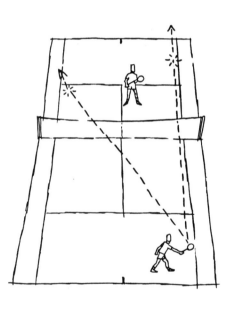

153

Play Deep Squares Against a Pusher

What to do against a player who merely pushes the ball back and simply waits for you to miss? Be patient. His strategy is based on making you impatient to get the point over with, hoping you will try for a winner at an inopportune moment.

Keep the ball in play until he gives you a short, easy ball, then carefully try for a winner or make a penetrating approach shot and advance to the net. In either case, play the ball carefully.

It might help you to divide the far end of your opponent's court into three large squares: deep forehand, deep center, and deep backhand. During a rally (when he's merely keeping the ball in play), merely keep the ball in play yourself by hitting every ball fairly easy (slow floaters are best) into one of these deep squares, waiting for a short ball from him. The short ball will eventually come—you merely have to outwait him—then deal with it.

Pushers don't try to *win* points; they merely wait for their opponents to *lose* points. Be patient when playing one; hit to the deep squares until you get the easy ball you want.

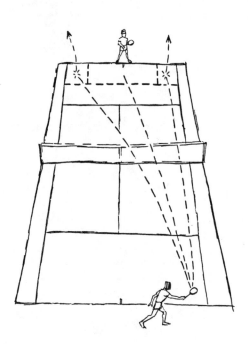

MISCELLANEOUS STROKES

You can control the degree of wrist action in your strokes—increasing it or decreasing it at will—by tightening or loosening your grip. The flexor muscles of the fingers—those you use to make a fist—pass over your wrist joint in such a manner that if you make a tight fist you automatically tighten up your wrist; if you merely curl your fingers into a loose fist, you have a loose wrist.

Make use of this anatomical fact to improve your strokes. If you want to hit with a firm wrist (the backhand ground stroke, for example), use a tight grip; if you want to hit with a lot of wrist action (the serve and the overhead), use a firm but not tight grip.

Vary the tightness of your grip to vary the degree of wrist action. Squeeze—and tighten the wrist—for control; squeeze much less—and loosen the wrist—for power.

154

Tighten Your Grip to Lock Your Wrist

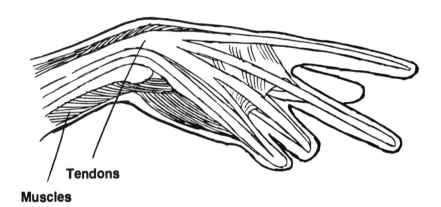

Tendons

Muscles

155

Be Careful with the Setups

One of the oldest axioms of tennis is: A good player rarely misses a setup; the mediocre player frequently does, and usually on critical points.

The mediocre player usually misses the setup because he gets careless with it. "It's easy," he thinks, "so I can be sloppy or spectacular with it," and he blows it! The good player, on the other hand, realizes that the setup is the ball he was hoping to get, the one he was waiting for, and he's not about to mess it up. He puts it away for a winner, but he plays it very carefully.

Be careful with the setups; look for them, pounce on them when you get them, but play them carefully. Don't take a chance on missing them by trying to be flashy or spectacular.

This looks easy, but I better be careful!!!

When playing with the wind blowing against you (toward you), try to use the wind rather than fight it.

In general, if the wind is strong, you can hit higher and harder than you can on a calm day. Your shots will be slowed down somewhat by the wind, so compensate for this by hitting higher and harder.

Scramble for all short shots, even if your first thought is that you won't get to the ball in time. These short shots will take long bounces because the wind will carry them a bit, so you'll be able to get to a lot of them if you scramble for them.

Aim your lobs to peak beyond the net, about midway between the net and the far service line. The wind will hold them back, and they'll drop more vertically than on a calm day, so aim them deeper than you normally do on a calm day.

Get well behind the bounce point of half lobs and slow floaters. They'll carry deep after the bounce, so get back quickly and far enough so they can fall down into your strike zone.

Toss the ball a little farther forward than you normally do when serving and let the wind carry it back to your normal serving point. If you toss to your normal serving point, the wind will carry the ball back behind you, forcing you to hit in an awkward and uncomfortable position.

Get well behind the bounce point of any lob you let bounce. The wind will carry the ball back, so be careful about letting the ball get behind your proper smashing point.

156

Make Adjustments When Playing Against the Wind

157

Adjust Your Game When Playing with the Wind

Be conscious of the wind at all times and make allowances for it in both your tactics and in your stroke production. Here are some suggestions for playing *with* the wind.

When your opponent gives you an easy, short ball, start quickly and immediately run as fast as you can as you scramble for it. The wind will cause this ball to die after the bounce, and, unless you hurry to the ball, you'll not get to it before it bounces twice.

Be careful on your approach and passing shots. The wind will add speed to them and they will carry over the baseline unless you play them carefully. Hit these balls a little easier than you would on a calm day; merely give them direction and let the wind add speed to them. If you can, hit them with topspin, too, to bring them down into the court.

Add a little spin to your serves. The wind tends to carry even a hard-hit serve, and, unless you make the ball hook or bend downward after it crosses the net, many of your serves will go long.

Use the drop shot and the drop volley sparingly. It is difficult to make these shots land close to the net, and the wind carries the ball after the bounce, causing a longer-than-usual bounce. Your opponent will be able to run down these long bouncers.

Let fairly high lobs bounce. The wind will cause them to bounce almost vertically and they'll be easy to smash then. Be careful to get directly below them, however, after they do bounce.

MISCELLANEOUS
STROKES

Outpsych
Your Opponent
by Taking Charge

Psychology plays an important role in many tennis matches. Often the winner of a match has really not beaten his opponent as much as he has outpsyched him. Here are some ways you can get the psychological edge on your opponents.

Be a take-charge player. Give your opponent the impression that you're in complete control of everything about the match. As you walk on the court to start the warm-up, you be the one to spin a racket, asking your opponent to call "rough or smooth" or "up or down." You be the one to measure the net, to check the placement of the singles sticks, to ask the umpire about ball-changing procedure, and to ask him who's calling what lines.

During the warm-up, ask your opponent if he wants some forehands, some backhands, or whatever. And ask him to give you forehands, backhands, volleys, and so on. Be the first to practice your serves, then be the first to say you're ready to play. Give him the impression that you really want to get the match started so you can start beating him.

During play be polite. Acknowledge his good shots, but don't compliment him too profusely. Pretend the match is fun (even if it isn't), that it's merely a good workout and that you're enjoying it immensely. Don't gripe or moan when you miss a shot; if you do, he'll think you're upset and he'll be encouraged.

Don't dawdle between points or during the changeover. Be the first one ready to play. Move briskly to retrieve balls and when getting in position to start a point.

159

Practice Your Weak Shots

Plan your practice sessions so that they are specific to your needs. Practice the things you can't do well. The tendency is to go out on the court and do the things you can already do well and to avoid the things that give you trouble. It's fun to make good shots—and it's very satisfying—so we want to make them all the time. And it's frustrating and annoying to make bad shots, so we tend to avoid the strokes that result in bad shots.

You *must* practice your weak shots. You'll become aggravated as you continue to miss them for a while, but only through regular, concentrated practice on them will you learn to make them.

Analyze your game, being as honest as you possibly can be about it, and determine your weaknesses. Then *practice* them.

MISCELLANEOUS STROKES

Learn to recover after making a shot, returning to the center of the court. Think of the center of the court (the area near the center mark) as home base and try to return to it.

Not always will you be able to return completely to home base, but at least try to. Start recovering immediately after you hit the ball (don't stand in place after you've hit it and watch it), and just as your opponent starts his backswing, make a ready-hop so that you are ready to move to his next shot. Even if you can return only partway, you'll have a better chance of getting to his next shot than if you had stayed off in the corner of the court somewhere.

160

Return to Home Base

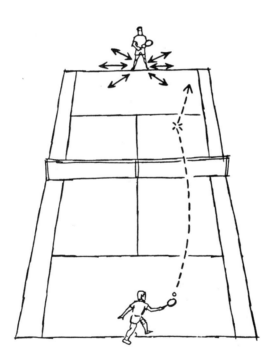

161

Hustle Back for Deep Balls

When your opponent is playing with a strong wind blowing from behind him, many of his deep, slow, floating shots will bounce higher and longer than they will under no-wind conditions. Unless you stay well behind these shots they will be difficult to play.

Anticipate a long, high bounce under these conditions, and position yourself accordingly. Hustle back quickly when you see the floater coming—the tendency is to go back too slowly—and get well behind the spot where you judge the ball will bounce, then let the wind blow the ball to you. Seldom will you go back too far; you can always move forward quickly at the last instant to adjust to the bounce. If you don't get back quickly enough, however, you'll have a difficult high shot to play.

MISCELLANEOUS
STROKES

Defense, though often overlooked, is an important part of successful tennis play. You must be able to scramble all over the court to return the ball, thus forcing your opponent to make several good shots rather than just one or two to win the point.

Practice scrambling to learn to hit while running, to learn to change directions quickly when running, and to learn to hit when you are off-balance while scrambling.

Practice with a partner. Stand about 2 or 3 feet behind your center mark and have him feed balls to you from his baseline. Ask him to feed balls quickly, one after the other, and to place them all over the court so that you have to scramble for them. Run for these balls, trying to get them all back. Repeated practice in this manner will improve your scrambling ability and your ability to play defense, and you'll be much tougher to beat.

162

Learn to Scramble to Play Defense

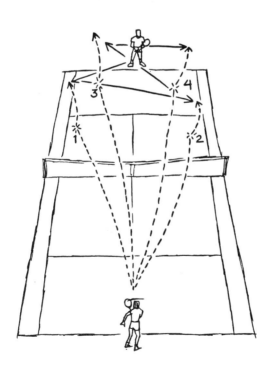

163

Run Like a <u>Runner</u> When Scrambling

Start your backswing early on normal shots to avoid any quick, jerky movements that could cause you to lose control over the racket. When you have to scramble for a ball, however, don't start your backswing so early that you have to run with your racket arm extending out to the side or behind you. You can't run fast and with good balance in this manner. Can you imagine a sprinter in a track meet running with one arm extended?

Run with a normal running motion, pumping your arms for speed and balance, and start your backswing as you get close to the ball. You'll get to a lot more balls by running like a runner.

MISCELLANEOUS
STROKES

When you are playing with a strong wind blowing from behind you (your opponent is hitting against the wind), you must start quickly and run fast when scrambling for a short ball. The wind will cause his short ball to take a shorter-than-normal bounce, and, unless you hurry to it with more-than-normal speed, you'll have difficulty getting to it before it bounces twice.

The secret in getting to these short balls is to make a fast start. As soon as you determine that the ball will be short, *sprint* to it, starting as fast as you can. Imagine that you are a sprinter in a track meet and that the short ball is the starter's gun. When you "hear" the gun (when you see the short ball), start quickly, then continue to sprint to the ball.

164

Sprint to Short Balls

165

Run
During the Warm-Up

Don't risk losing the first few games of a match by not being warmed up sufficiently. Use the period the way it is intended to be used; get yourself warmed up and ready to play. Tune up your strokes, but tune up your body, too.

Start the period by hitting ground strokes, but don't run for balls that are not fairly close to you. Play only those balls that you don't have to move more than a few feet for. Don't run hard, and don't make any vigorous swings or moves. Move up to the net position after a few minutes of ground stroke practice and practice a few volleys.

Move back to the baseline area and again hit ground strokes, but gradually begin to run for balls that don't come close to you. Pick up the speed at which you run and pretend you are actually playing points. A few minutes spent running for balls like this will get you ready to practice your serves and overhead smashes. Swing easily at first as you practice these strokes; they require strenuous moves that could cause muscle tears or joint injuries if your body is not ready to make these moves.

Start the match only when you feel that you are ready to play all-out even for the first few points. If you get off to a good start, your chances of winning the match are much better than if you waste the first few games by not being warmed up.

MISCELLANEOUS
STROKES

When your opponent lobs when you are at the net and you have to go back only a few steps to smash the ball, you can get back easily by turning sideways and skipping back. When he lobs deep and the lob clears you, however, and you are forced to let the ball bounce and go back and play a defensive ground stroke, you won't get back in time if you try to skip back. You must run back for these shots.

As soon as you determine that the ball will clear you and that you will not be able to smash it, turn to face the rear fence and run back, watching the ball over your shoulder so that it doesn't hit you. Run fast, trying not to let the ball get behind you.

Think of going back for these clearing lobs as being similar to the way an outfielder in baseball goes back to chase down a fly ball that clears him. You'll get back fast if you go back this way, and you'll probably be able to chase down the lob. Be sure to run to the side of the ball, too, so that you can make a sideways swing at it.

166

Run Back
Like an Outfielder
for Deep Lobs

TACTICS FOR DOUBLES

Tactics for successful doubles play are based on the idea that doubles is a *team* game and that players play together as a *team*. If you and your partner understand the principles of successful play and work together as a team, you will enjoy much more success than if you were to play without regard to these principles.

Several principles of successful play are offered in this section for various levels of play. Learn to apply them and you will improve your doubles skills.

When serving from the right court in doubles, stand five or six feet to the right of the center mark. From this position you can place your serve to the receiver's backhand or hit it wide to his forehand. And, after the serve, you will be in good position to return any ball hit wide to your alley or, if you follow your serve to the net, to make a forehand volley.

When serving from the left court, stand about in the middle of your side of the court. From here you can serve to the receiver's backhand, forcing him to make a difficult cross-court shot to keep the ball away from your partner at the net. You will also be in a good position to play any balls hit wide to your backhand alley, and you will often be able to run around balls hit slightly to your backhand side to play them with your stronger forehand stroke. In addition, if you follow your serve to the net, you will be able to play many service returns with a forehand volley.

167

When Serving, Stand Near the Middle of Your Court

168

**Returning the Serve:
Use the Center Strap
as a Guide**

Learn to use the center strap as a guide when returning the serve in doubles, hitting the ball to either side of the strap, and you'll seldom have to worry about an active net man cutting off your returns.

Aim your returns a foot or so to the side of the strap (to your left when receiving in the right court, to your right when receiving in the left court). Even a *very* active net man will have trouble getting to these balls in time to deal with them effectively.

As you hit these balls, pretend that the court into which you are hitting is short and that your ball must land near the service line or at least well inside the baseline. This will force you to keep the ball low, making your returns even more difficult for your opponents to handle.

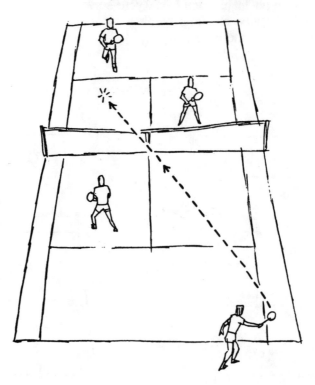

*TACTICS
FOR DOUBLES*

When one of your opponents serves to you and rushes to the net in doubles, he is, for a brief instant, in the midcourt area commonly referred to as "the danger zone" or "no man's land." Exploit his weakness of position by aiming your return of serve at his feet. Try to force him to hit a low volley or a half volley, which he'll have to hit up (and easy) and which your partner at the net can pounce on and slash away for a winner.

You don't have to hit your return of serve hard; you want to get the ball low, above all, and even an easy shot that is low is a good one. The ideal shot, though, is a hard one at his feet.

This low shot will quite often cause your opponent to pop up his return; your partner should be able to deal with this pop-up easily.

169

Returning the Serve: Hit to the Server's Feet

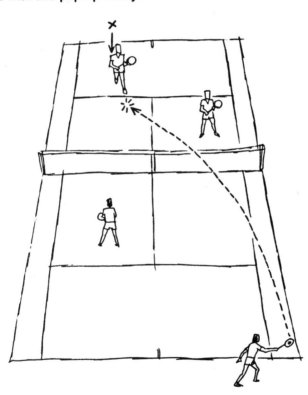

170

**Protect Your Alley
When Playing Net**

Your primary responsibility at the net is to protect your alley. You should be eager to cut off any cross-court returns or slow floaters you can reach, but, above all, let nothing go past you down the alley.

To cover your alley, you should move slightly toward the alley when your opponent is forced to hit from wide in the court. How far you should move depends upon how far your opponent moves. If he is forced very wide, well beyond his alley, you should move well to the side of your normal net position toward your alley.

While protecting your alley, be ready to take advantage of any poorly hit cross-court shot. Step toward the ball and, if you can reach it, volley it either at the opposing net man's feet or through the opening between your opponents.

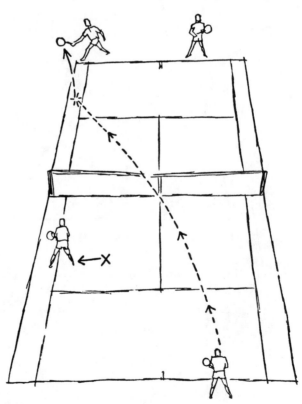

TACTICS
FOR DOUBLES

The volleying position is generally the attacking position in doubles; both teams try to get there as quickly and as safely as they can. Quite often, however, a doubles team finds itself caught in the one-up, one-back position.

If you get caught in this position and you are hitting from deep in the court, follow the cardinal principle of "hit in front of your partner." By hitting in front of your partner, you will force your opponent to make a difficult cross-court shot away from your partner who is at the net. If this cross-court shot is not accurately placed, your partner can cut it off and slash it away for a winner.

Hit in Front of Your Partner

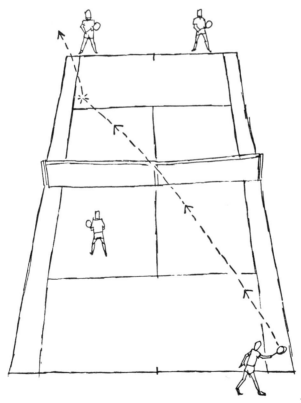

172

Cover Up
for Your Partner

Play as a *team* in doubles; learn to cover up for your partner. If he is forced wide to play a ball, either at the net or in the backcourt, the opening between the two of you will be increased; move to make this opening smaller, covering up for him. If he is forced wide to the right, move to the right also; if he is forced wide to the left, move to the left. As you move one way or the other, you'll leave a little opening on the side opposite the direction you're moving (on your left if you move right, on your right if you move left), but creating this small opening is clearly better than leaving a large opening between you and your partner.

Move as a team; cover up for him and expect him to cover up for you. Such teamwork is essential for effective doubles play.

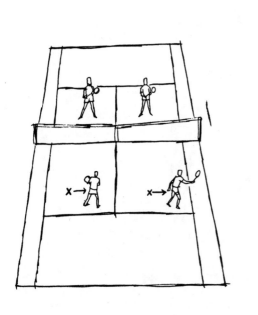 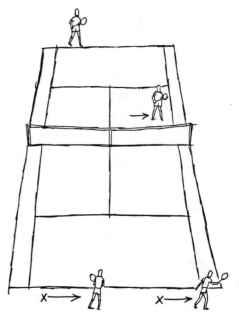

When you are in the backcourt in doubles, do you and your partner frequently get confused about whether or not to go to the net after hitting a relatively short ball? Does one of you go up, assuming the other will go up also, only to find that the other decided to stay back?

You can end this confusion by following a cardinal rule: The hitter decides whether both players should go up or stay back. He knows better than the other player how difficult his shot is. If he feels that he can make a forceful return, he should follow the return to the net, and his partner should go up with him; if he can't make a forceful return, he should stay back, and his partner should stay back with him. In either case, the hitter should decide whether the team should go up or stay back, and his partner should react accordingly.

Let the Hitter Decide When to Go Up

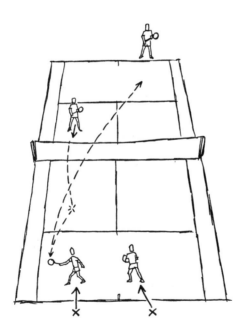

174

Set the Ball Up for Your Partner

Think of doubles as a *team* game, which it is, and try to make your teammate look good by setting balls up for him.

You can do this by *not* trying to win the point by yourself by going for the big shot all the time. Go for the big shot only when you are absolutely certain you can pull it off. If you're not sure you can pull it off, forget it and merely try to force your opponents to make a weak shot that your partner can put away. Usually a low shot to the feet of your opponents will result in a weak return; at worse, such a low ball will prevent your partner from being put on the spot.

Be a cagey teammate. Maneuver your opponents out of position or force them to make weak shots so that *your partner* can finish off the rally. This will make you and your partner a better team, and you'll be in demand as a doubles partner.

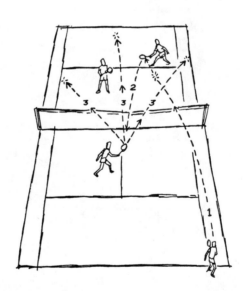

In high-level doubles play, all four players should try to get to the net as quickly as possible because the net is the attacking position.

The server's partner should be at the net as the server serves, standing 8 or 9 feet from the net and about 1 foot inside the singles sideline. The server should follow his serve to the net, going forward to join his partner in the attacking position. Each player should then cover one side of the court.

The receiver of the serve should try to return the serve to the feet of the net-rushing server. His partner should play either on the service line, the baseline, or in the normal net position, depending upon how well the receiver can return the serve.

If the serve can be returned without too much difficulty, the receiver's partner should play on the service line or forward of it so that he can move up quickly and pounce on the weak first shot made by the opponents. If the serve is difficult to handle, the receiver's partner can play on the baseline; should his partner make a bad return of serve and give the opponents an easy ball, he won't be in a vulnerable position.

175

Advanced Doubles: Get to the Net

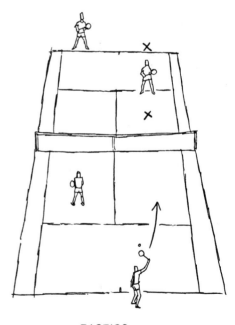

176

Change Your Waiting Grip When at the Net

When your partner is serving from the right of the center mark in singles or doubles, you should be at the net very close to the singles sideline. Because the receiver of the serve will try to keep the ball away from you, he'll aim cross-court, to your right. If his shot is not accurately placed, you should be able to cut if off with a forehand volley. Be prepared for this shot by using the forehand grip as your waiting grip.

When your partner serves from the left of the center mark and you're at the net on the right side of the court, most of the receiver's shots will be cross-court to your backhand side. Be prepared for these by using your backhand grip as your waiting grip.

Change your waiting grips, depending upon which side you are playing on when at the net, and you'll be better prepared to deal with the majority of returns.

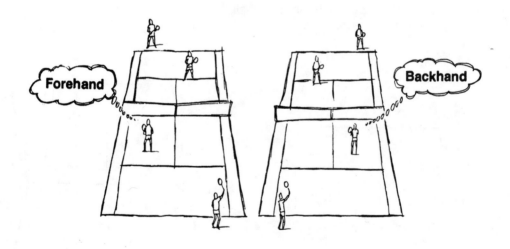

If you and your partner are inexperienced players, you should use the both-back method when receiving the serve in doubles. With both of you on the baseline, the receiver is not forced to make a low return in order to protect his partner at the net. He merely has to keep the ball away from the server's partner (who is at the net), playing a relatively easy-to-make slow floater.

When you are in the both-back position, let the player who is in the left court play balls that are hit down the middle between the two of you. He can play these balls with his forehand.

If either of you is forced to run forward to play a short ball, the other player should run forward, too. Both of you will then be in the forecourt, in the attacking position, and you can slash the next return at the opposing net man or between him and his partner.

177

Both of You Play Back When Receiving the Serve

CONDITIONING AND STRENGTH FOR TENNIS

One of the basic requirements for success in tennis is a good deal of strength in the hitting hand, the wrist, the forearm, and the shoulder. Strength is required to overcome the resistance of the fast-moving ball and to enable you to move the racket quickly and with speed so that you can add power to your strokes.

You can develop strength through constant and regular play. This takes time, however, and the necessary strength will be developed slowly. To hasten the development, do the exercises suggested in this section. They require virtually no expensive equipment, they take only a short period of time to perform, and they can be done off the court during your leisure time.

Prepare for the tennis season by building strength in your hand, wrist, and forearm. Strength in these areas is necessary if you are to hit with speed and control and ward off wrist and arm fatigue in long matches.

Do the following exercises regularly (about three times a week):

1. Stretch the fingers of your hitting hand, then make a tight fist, alternately. Do this 50 times the first few days, then 75 times, then do 100 regularly.

2. Hold the corner of a double sheet of newspaper in your hitting hand, holding your hand away from your body. Try to roll the newspaper into a tight ball, using only your hand and fingers. Do this until your hand is tired.

3. Place a rubber band across the back of your hitting hand, looping it around your little finger and your thumb. Then try to work the rubber band off your hand using only your fingers. Keep trying until your hand gets tired.

Do Preseason Exercises for Strength

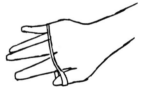

179

**Exercise for Strength
During the Season**

You can use an old bicycle inner tube, obtained free from any bike shop, to develop the strength necessary for successful play. Cut the valve from the tube, tie a knot in each end of the tube, then use the tube as shown in the diagrams.

Start with your hands far enough apart so there is a good deal of slack in the tube. Later, after you have developed some strength, start with your hands closer together so there is less slack in the tube; this will provide more resistance and develop more strength. Do these exercises regularly *after* playing or before retiring in the evening.

CONDITIONING
AND STRENGTH
FOR TENNIS

1. Hold a heavy book in your hitting hand. Rest your forearm palm down on a table with your hand and the book hanging over the edge of the table. Keep your forearm on the table and raise and lower the book by bending your wrist up and down until your arm gets tired. Then turn your forearm so that your palm is facing up; again raise and lower the book until your arm gets tired.
2. Hold a heavy book in your hitting hand and let your arm hang straight down so that the book rests against the outside of your right thigh. Keeping your arm straight, raise the book to shoulder level, then lower it to your thigh. Continue raising and lowering the book until your arm gets tired.
3. Hold a heavy book in your hitting hand as you simulate the swings of the various strokes, swinging as though you were hitting forehand and backhand ground strokes, the serve, and forehand and backhand volleys.

180

Continue to Develop Strength

181

Use an Inner Tube to Develop Strength

You can develop strength for tennis by using an old bicycle inner tube as you simulate your forehand and backhand swings. Tie one end of the tube to a net post as shown in the diagrams; grasp the other end of the tube with your hitting hand and s-t-r-e-t-c-h the tube as you swing your arm and hand in the shape of your normal swings.

You can also do this one at home: Tie a big knot in one end of the tube, fling this end through a partially open door and quickly close the door so that the knotted end of the tube is outside the door while the unknotted end is inside. Grasp the unknotted end and stretch the tube as you swing in the shape of your ground strokes.

1   2   3

3   2   1

CONDITIONING
AND STRENGTH
FOR TENNIS

To play successfully, you must be able to start running quickly, stop quickly, change directions as you make short dashes over the court, and recover from off-balance and out-of-court positions. You must be quick and agile. Here are some exercises that will help you develop quickness and agility. Do them regularly.

Crab walk

Reverse crab walk

Knee jump

Spread jump

Touch jump

Burpees

Jump through

183

Exercises for Flexibility

Because you must twist, bend, leap, and stretch to play active tennis, your body and muscles must be loose, supple, and flexible. Not only will you play better if you are loose and flexible, but you'll probably be able to ward off injury better as well.

Here are several simple exercises that, if done regularly, will condition your body so that it can respond successfully to the rigorous demands of the game.

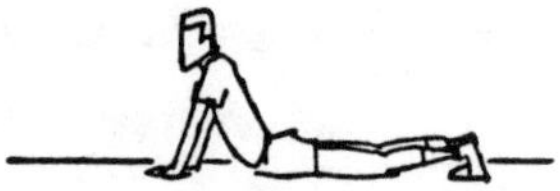

Seal stretch

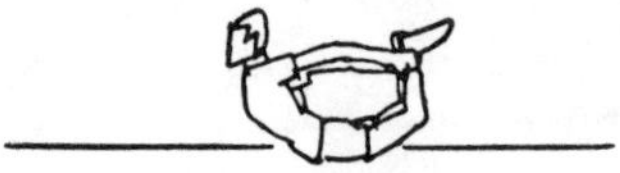

Back basket

Chin to heels

Heels over head

Thigh stretch

Toe stretch

Toe touch

Situp V

Flutters

CONDITIONING AND STRENGTH FOR TENNIS

You can build up your endurance by engaging in a number of on-court running drills. Several drills are listed below. As you go through the drills, pretend you are actually running to get to a ball as you would in actual play. Start all drills at home base (about three feet behind the center mark).

Use On-Court Running Drills to Develop Endurance

- Run forward toward the net, stop quickly near the net, then run backward toward the rear fence. Stop near the fence and run forward again. Keep running forward and backward, stopping and changing direction quickly.
- Run to the right to the singles sideline, stop quickly and run to the left to the other sideline, stop and change direction again. Continue running left and right.
- Run forward diagonally to the right (as if to play a short forehand), then backward, then forward to the left (as if to play a short backhand), then backward again.
- Scramble all over the court (forward, backward, left, right) as though you were being run all over the court by an opponent.

185

Play Shadow Tennis to Develop Endurance

The best way to develop endurance for tennis is to tire yourself in practice by making the same movements you make during play. During play you must start running quickly and run fast, you must stop abruptly and change directions quickly, and you must lunge, leap, twist, turn, and stretch.

Practice these moves by playing shadow tennis. Select any open space with adequate room and pretend you are playing points. Run left and right, forward and backward as quickly as you can as if you were scrambling all over a tennis court during a point. Run until you get tired, then rest for 10 or 12 seconds and run again. Continue doing this kind of running, twisting, and turning well beyond the first signs of fatigue and you will gradually develop great endurance.

Jogging and rope skipping help to develop endurance, but in play you don't run slowly for a long time, nor do you bounce up and down in one place. Plainly, jogging and rope skipping are not much like what you do on the court during play. The moves you make when you play shadow tennis should be identical to the moves you make when you play; shadow tennis will then be a much more effective way to develop endurance.

Avoid
Cramps and Fatigue

Your body loses a lot of water and other elements (potassium, magnesium, sodium, and calcium) through perspiration during play. An excessive loss of these elements could lead to muscle cramps and general fatigue. Many players take salt pills while playing to prevent cramps and fatigue. Try taking these pills; they might be helpful to you.

If you can't take pills—some people get nauseated from them—try drinking one of the many commercial products (Gatorade, E.R.G., Brake Time, Quick Kick) that are designed to replace the lost elements. Not all experts who study the effects of exercise on the body agree that these products are as beneficial as their manufacturers claim. Maybe they won't provide you with quick energy and help to ward off cramps, but they will quench your thirst and will probably give you a mental and psychological boost as well.

CONDITIONING
AND STRENGTH
FOR TENNIS

THE
RULES

Several variations of scoring have become part of the official rules of tennis in recent years, and many players are confused about them. These variations are explained simply for you here so that there should be no confusion in *your* mind about how they work.

Included here, also, are some tips on some little-known or often confused or misunderstood rules. Become familiar with them; they can sometimes help you gain a slight advantage over your opponent. The least they can do is make you a more knowledgeable player.

The winner of the toss (the spin) has three choices: (1) he can choose to serve or receive, (2) he can choose to start play in the north or south court, or (3) he can choose not to choose and make his opponent choose either to serve or receive or to play in the north or south court.

If a player chooses to serve or receive, the other player has the option of starting in the north or south court. If a player chooses to start on the north or south court, the other player has the option of serving or receiving.

Choose number 3 above the next time you win the toss. It's not often done, and perhaps your opponent will be so befuddled by your choice that you'll wind up with your preferred selection of serving or receiving *and* the north or south court.

187

Choose Side or Serve, or Make Him Choose

Right side up—*I* serve; upside down—*you* receive!

188

Put the Singles Sticks in the Right Place

Most courts you play on will be lined for doubles play, and the net posts will be permanently set for doubles. When you play singles on this kind of court, singles sticks are—or should be—used to raise the net to its proper height near the singles sidelines.

Where should you place the sticks? Three feet outside the singles sidelines (the permanent posts are three feet outside the doubles sidelines).

There's a convenient way to measure this three-foot distance: one racket length and one racket width. (It's the same way you measure the height of the net at the center line before you start play.)

Simply lay the rackets on the court, extending out from the outside edge of the singles sideline—one length and one width—to determine where the sticks should be placed. Put the sticks in place and the net will be the regulation height.

The rules permit you and your partner to change the order of serving at the start of a new set in doubles. If you have a stronger serve than your partner, you can serve first for your team in the new set even though you were the last to serve in the previous set.

Similarly, you can change the order of receiving at the start of a new set. If you received in the forehand court (the right court) during the first set, you and your partner can change places so that *he* receives in the forehand court during the second set.

If you and your partner do not do well in the first set of a match, take advantage of this rule and perhaps you'll do better in the next set.

189

Change the Order of Serving or Receiving

190

Reach Over the Net to Play a Backward-Bouncing Ball

You are permitted to reach over the net to play a ball, actually making contact with the ball on your opponent's side of the net, *only* when the ball is bouncing backward over the net. Be careful when reaching over, however, because you are not allowed to touch the net with your racket, body, or clothing.

If the ball has not bounced, you must make contact with it on your side of the net. You are allowed to follow through over the net, however, provided you do not touch the net.

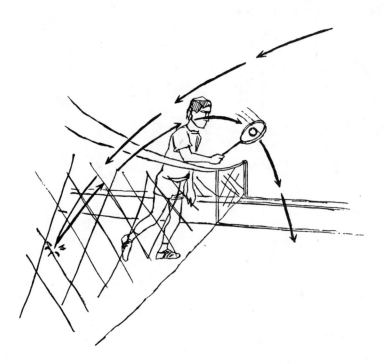

You can avoid long, drawn-out sets by playing a 9-point tie-breaker game when the score is tied at 6 games all—the player who wins 5 points wins the tie-breaker game and the set (7 games to 6).

If it's your turn to serve the tie-breaker game, you serve points (1) and (2), right and left; your opponent then serves (3) and (4), right and left, after which you and he change ends. You then serve (5) and (6), right and left, and he serves (7) and (8), right and left. If the score reaches 4 points all, you (the receiver) have the option of making your opponent serve (9) (the sudden-death point) from either the right or left.

The player who serves the first point in a tie-breaker game becomes the receiver for the first game of the next set.

191

Shorten the Match with the 9-Point Tie-Breaker

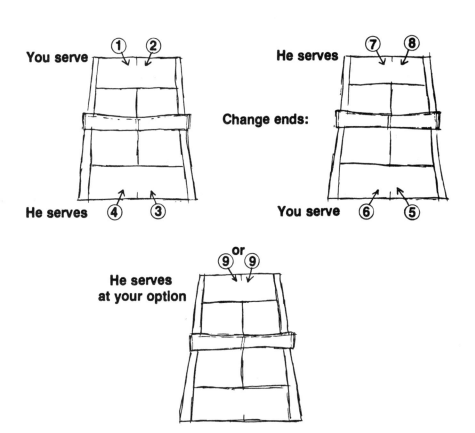

You serve ① ②

He serves ⑦ ⑧

Change ends:

He serves ④ ③

You serve ⑥ ⑤

or
⑨ ⑨

He serves
at your option

192

Save Time with the 12-Point Tie-Breaker

When your score is tied at 6 games all, you can determine the winner of the set by playing a 12-point tie-breaker game—the first player to win 7 points or more and be ahead by 2 points wins the game and the set (7 games to 6).

If it's your turn to serve the tie-breaker game, you serve point (1) from the right court; your opponent then serves points (2) and (3), left and right. You serve (4) and (5), left and right; he serves (6), left. You and he then change ends and he serves (7), right. You serve (8) and (9), left and right; he serves (10) and (11), left and right; and you serve (12), left.

If points reach 6 all (no one has yet won 7 points), you change ends and continue as before (you serve (13), right; he serves (14) and (15), left and right, etc.) until one of you gets ahead by 2 points and wins the game and the set. You then change ends and your opponent serves first to start the new set.

During the tie-breaker game points are called: "zero-one," "zero-two," "one-two," and so on.

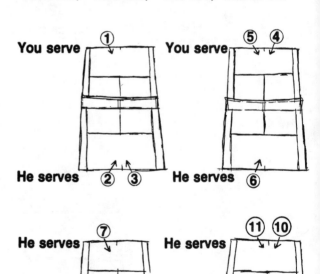

If you're tired of long, drawn-out games in which the score goes from deuce to ad to deuce to ad, use the no-ad scoring method.

In no-ad a player needs to win only four points to win a game. Points are called love, 15, 30, 40, game, or zero, 1, 2, 3, game, whichever you prefer. If the score reaches 40 all (or 3 all), the next point is game point for both players; at 40 all (or 3 all) the receiver has his choice of receiving the serve in either the right or left court.

The no-ad method is a good one to combine with a 9-point tie-breaker (when games reach 6 all) to shorten matches. If you are limited in court time, you can play many more games during your allotted time by using this method than you could if you were to use the conventional scoring method.

193

Use No-Ad Scoring to Shorten the Match

MISCELLANEOUS TIPS AND SUGGESTIONS

If you're really serious about becoming a good tennis player, become a student of the game. Make a special effort to study and learn everything you can about it.

Subscribe to one or more of the many fine tennis magazines that are now published. Most of them are issued monthly. They contain articles on stroking techniques (often extremely well illustrated), tactics, strategy, conditioning, training, and so on, all written by knowledgeable teachers or coaches. They'll also keep you abreast of all the latest developments and happenings in the game. You can read about tournament results, rule changes, new equipment—anything that's pertinent to the game.

Talk tennis with any good player or teacher who's willing to talk with you about it (you'll find most of them more than happy to share their ideas and concepts with you). Ask them questions about whatever problems you're having, and ask for suggestions for solving these problems. Don't expect a free lesson, however; their time and expertise is valuable. Most of them will give you some free advice, though, if you approach them in the right way and don't make a nuisance of yourself.

194

Become a Student of the Game

195

Play Under Safe Conditions

Tennis is not a dangerous game; the chances of your getting hurt during play are very slim. Nevertheless, you should take certain safety precautions.

Keep the playing area and the area beyond the baseline and the sideline clear of all objects. Place racket covers, towels, sweaters, ball cans, etc., against a net post.

Close all gates and doors to avoid the danger of running into partially open ones.

Stop play if the court becomes even the least bit wet. Certain court surfaces become slippery after even only a few drops of rain have fallen on them.

Never hit a ball or throw a racket in anger. Control your emotions. Shout a warning if there is danger of a thrown or hit ball hitting someone.

Tie shoe laces securely, leaving no loose ends, to avoid tripping while you run. Wear shoes and socks that fit to avoid blisters. Wear clean, loose-fitting clothing suitable for the weather.

Stay on your own court during play. Don't go into an adjacent court to retrieve balls; ask players on that court to return your balls to you.

If one of your foursome fails to show up some-day and you have an hour or so of court time assigned to you, play three-man singles. It's a game that will keep all three of you active be-cause nobody sits out for any great length of time, and it's fun. Here's how it works:

Players A and B oppose Player X, with A and B alternating serves as they play as a team. Player A serves the first point while B stands off court; B serves and plays the second point while A stands off court. Player A plays the third point, B plays the fourth, and so on until the game is completed. Player X, of course, receives all serves.

In the second game, B serves and plays the first point, A serves and plays the second, B plays the third, and so on.

After the second game A changes places with X; B and X then play two games against A. When two more games are completed, B changes places with A, and A and X play two games against B.

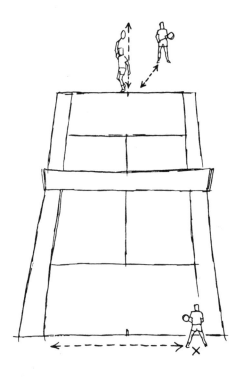

197

Learn by Watching <u>Good</u> Players

If you are a beginner, you can become familiar with the idea of the game and the basic strokes used to play it by watching good players. Spend some time at your local courts, being sure to watch good players, or, better still, watch one of the many tennis matches that now appear regularly on TV.

As you watch, concentrate on the players; don't watch the ball. The tendency when watching tennis matches is to follow the ball with your eyes and to get emotionally involved in the game. This is fine if you're watching for entertainment, but if you're watching to learn about the game, watch the players. Notice everything you can about them; you'll be surprised how much you can learn by watching their strokes, footwork, tactics, and strategy.

*MISCELLANEOUS
TIPS AND
SUGGESTIONS*

198

Use the Right Racket

Because of the many different kinds of rackets now available, selecting the kind you think is best for you can be a bewildering task.

You can choose one made of wood, steel, aluminum, graphite, fiberglass, or several other materials. The choice is yours, depending upon your preference; they all have good and bad qualities.

More important than the material of which the racket is made is its weight and grip size. Rackets are usually marked with little stick-on tags (usually located on the side of the handle just above the leather grip) that indicate their general weight classifications and grip sizes. Letters (L, M, H) indicate whether a racket is light, medium, or heavy; numbers (4¼, 4½, etc.) indicate its grip size in inches.

Here's a general guide for selecting a racket: L, 4¼-4½: suitable for young children, girls, and women. M, 4½-4⅝: suitable for strong teenagers, strong women, most men. H, 4¾-4⅞: suitable for strong, big men.

199

Match a New Racket to Your Old One

Selecting a new racket to replace an old one can be a problem. It's difficult to match the new one to your old one in weight and balance because the new one will be without strings as you make some practice swings with it in the sporting goods store. You'll have no way of knowing how it will feel after it is strung.

You can make an unstrung racket feel like a strung one by attaching a ¾ oz. weight to the head of it (a ¾ oz. bait casting practice plug is ideal for this; you can get one in the fishing department of most sporting goods stores).

Fix the weight to a large rubber band then stretch the rubber band across the center of the racket head. The unstrung racket will now have approximately the same weight and balance as it would if it were strung.

Try the weight on several different frames as you make some practice swings with them until you find one that matches your old one.

It is practically impossible to develop good, sound tennis strokes if you play with old, light, worn-out balls. When the outer layer of fuzz is worn off a ball, the ball will simply not go where you hit it; it will sail and float wildly when hit. The fuzz on a good ball serves the same purpose that feathers on an arrow do; it keeps the ball going where you aimed it.

When you buy balls, be sure you buy the ones that are packed under pressure in a sealed can (three to a can), and be sure, too, that they are marked "heavy duty" or "extra duty." These balls will retain their inside pressure and stay lively longer than will balls packaged in cellophane. There is a no-pressure ball on the market, however, that does stay lively.

You can buy white, yellow, or red balls. Because they are more visible than the others, yellow balls are the most popular.

200

Buy Pressure-Packed Balls

201

Wear the Right Clothing

For a long time white was the traditional—and often the required—color for tennis clothing. Color has now become the vogue, however, and you can wear just about anything as long as it's neat, clean, and in good taste.

Shorts and shirts for men, dresses or shorts and tops for women are standard. Warm-up suits or sweat suits have become extremely popular in recent years; they are worn before and after play and during play on cool days. A cap or visor, to keep the sun out of your eyes, is often worn, too.

Soft rubber-soled shoes complete the tennis uniform. The low-cut sneaker type worn over fairly heavy socks (to prevent blisters) is best.

A sweaty palm can cause serious gripping problems on a hot, humid day. To prevent this, there are several things you can do.

Avoid a Slippery Grip

- Rub a commercial antiperspirant on your hitting palm an hour or so before you play.
- Wear an absorbent "Swet-Let" on your hitting wrist to keep the perspiration on your forearm from running down into your palm.
- Get some sawdust from your local lumber company (they'll give it to you free) and carry a pocketful of it when you play. Bounce a handful of it around in the palm of your hitting hand between points to keep your palm dry.
- Carry a small towel with you during play. Tuck it into the waistband of your shorts on your left hip and use it to dry your hand between points.
- Check the leather grip on your racket. Leather gets slimy and slippery after being used for a while. If your grip is slippery, replace it with a new one.

203

**Deal Carefully
with Injuries**

Tennis is not a dangerous game, but injuries sometimes do occur. You should be aware of effective ways to deal with the more common ones.

Sunburn. Avoid continued exposure to the sun. If severe, apply a sterile gauze dressing and see a physician.

Heat Exhaustion. Weakness, with profuse sweating, indicates state of shock due to depletion of salt and water. Lie in the shade with your head lower than or level with your body. Sip salt water. Obtain medical care at once.

Bruise. Apply ice bag or cold cloths, and rest the injured muscle. Protect from further aggravation. If severe, see a physician.

Cramp. Sit or lie down and rest the cramped limb. If cramp occurs on a hot day, sip salt water.

Strain and Sprain. Elevate the injured part and apply an ice bag or cold cloths. Apply a pressure bandage to reduce the swelling. Avoid putting weight on it and obtain medical care.

Nosebleed. Sit or stand. Cover the nose with cold cloths. If bleeding is heavy, pinch the nose and place small cotton pack in the nostril.

Blisters. Keep clean with mild soap and water. Do not aggravate further. If broken, trim ragged edges with sterile equipment.

Dislocation. Support the joint. Apply an ice bag or cold cloths to reduce the swelling, and see a physician at once.

*MISCELLANEOUS
TIPS AND
SUGGESTIONS*